A Compact Guide to Discovering God's Will

Gordon S. Jackson

NAVPRESS

A Compact Guide
to Discovering
God's Will

Gordon S. Jackson

NAVPRESS

Bringing Truth to Life
P.O. Box 35001, Colorado Springs, Colorado 80935

OUR GUARANTEE TO YOU

We believe so strongly in the message of our books that we are making this quality guarantee to you. If for any reason you are disappointed with the content of this book, return the title page to us with your name and address and we will refund to you the list price of the book. To help us serve you better, please briefly describe why you were disappointed. Mail your refund request to: NavPress, P.O. Box 35002, Colorado Springs, CO 80935.

The Navigators is an international Christian organization. Our mission is to reach, disciple, and equip people to know Christ and to make Him known through successive generations. We envision multitudes of diverse people in the United States and every other nation who have a passionate love for Christ, live a lifestyle of sharing Christ's love, and multiply spiritual laborers among those without Christ.

NavPress is the publishing ministry of The Navigators. NavPress publications help believers learn biblical truth and apply what they learn to their lives and ministries. Our mission is to stimulate spiritual formation among our readers.

Library of Congress Catalog Card Number: 2001032974
ISBN 1-57683-256-2

Cover design by Ray Moore
Series Editor: Brad Lewis
Creative Team: Marla Kennedy, Terry Behimer, Glynese Northam

Some of the anecdotal illustrations in this book are true to life and are included with the permission of the persons involved. All other illustrations are composites of real situations, and any resemblance to people living or dead is coincidental.

Unless otherwise identified, all Scripture quotations in this publication are taken from the HOLY BIBLE: NEW INTERNATIONAL VERSION® (NIV®). Copyright © 1973, 1978, 1984 by International Bible Society. Used by permission of Zondervan Publishing House. All rights reserved. Other versions used include: *The Jerusalem Bible* (JB), © 1985 by Darton, Longman & Todd, Ltd., and Doubleday & Company, Inc.; extracts from the *Revised English Bible* (REV) © Oxford University Press and Cambridge University Press 1989.

Jackson, Gordon, 1949-
    A compact guide to discovering God's will / Gordon S. Jackson.
        p. cm.
    Includes bibliographical references and index.
    ISBN 1-57683-256-2
    1. Christian life. 2. Providence and government of God. 3. God--Will. I. Title.
BV4509.5 .J33 2001
45.4--dc21   2001032974

FOR A FREE CATALOG OF
NAVPRESS BOOKS & BIBLE STUDIES,
CALL 1-800-366-7788 (USA)
OR 1-416-499-4615 (CANADA)

Printed in the United States of America

1 2 3 4 5 6 7 8 9 10 / 05 04 03 02 01

For Kathleen and Winston

Contents

Acknowledgments

This book has its genesis in the countless conversations I have had with Whitworth College students over nearly two decades, as they have sought answers to the kinds of questions that I've tried answering in the pages that follow. Although they didn't realize it at the time, they prodded me into taking on this project with their questions about whether to major in this subject or that, or whether to take this internship or that. At times the range of their concerns went beyond academic issues to hard questions they faced in their personal lives. So, more than anyone, it's my students to whom I owe much gratitude.

Special thanks also are due to the following friends and colleagues who generously gave of their time to critique this book as it took shape: Mildred Basing, Jim Edwards, Carl Green, Karen Harrison, Dick Mandeville, Greg Orwig, Hannah Vahlstrom, and Carrie Wasser. In addition, my daughter, Sarah, and my wife, Sue, also made various suggestions while I worked on this project—some of them even related to the book. Sarah and my son, Matthew, also helped proofread the manuscript. My secretary at Whitworth College, Martha Brown, merits recognition for her computer wizardry that helped me prepare the manuscript.

Lastly, a word of appreciation is due to the many authors on whose work I have relied in writing this Compact Guide. The books and booklets that I've found most helpful are included in the section on "Resources" (p. 186). Several of these publications have given me great encouragement and direction in my own quest for guidance. I hope this volume will provide you with similar encouragement and direction as you make godly choices. To the extent that this book helps you do that, this project represents my thank you to those who, through their writings on guidance, have made an immeasurable impact on helping me think through God's leading at key points in my life.

A Guidance Road Map

What's the Issue?	Where to Turn (assuming you've already read The Big Five, pages 17, 23-25)
How should I approach a guidance issue in my life?	Topics 1-6, 7, 8, 9, 15, 17, 22, 23, 24, 25, 26, 55
How does God guide and what should I expect in the guidance process?	Topics 10, 11
How can I be confident that God will guide me?	Topic 18
What is my part in the guidance process?	Topics 12, 13, 14, 19, 21, 47, 57
How can I be confident that God *has* guided me?	Topic 58
How can I know if God is calling me to a particular ministry, task, or job?	Topics 44, 45, 46
What should I bear in mind when I need to make a decision?	Topics 16, 29, 31, 33, 34, 35, 36, 41
How can I know when I should wait?	Topic 40

What's the Issue?	Where to Turn (assuming you've already read The Big Five)
How can I separate my motives from what God wants?	Topics 38, 43, 54
How does God want me to choose between two or more alternative options?	Topics 20, 30
How does God want me to move ahead when I have no idea where to turn next?	Topic 42
How can I stop worrying about making the wrong choice?	Topics 48, 52, 56
What if I have to make a decision in a hurry?	Topic 37
What common mistakes do people make when seeking guidance?	Topics 27, 28, 32, 39, 49, 50, 51, 53
What if I've made a mistake in understanding guidance?	Topic 59
Where will I find prayers on guidance?	Topic 61
Where can I get further information?	Topics 60, 62

Introduction

Choosing Well: Living Out God's Will

Most of the time in our Christian walk, we already know perfectly well what God's will is and what He expects of us. It is to continue the work He's already given us, precisely where we are, according to the guidelines for godly living we know from Scripture. But there come moments when we face major decisions, crossroads in our journey where the signposts aren't as legible or well lit as we would like. We face hard choices. Should I attend college X or college Y? Should I marry this person, or not? Should I move an aged parent into a long-term care facility? Should I take that job in Cleveland? Should I leave an increasingly fractious church or stay on as a healer? Some are decisions that we've anticipated for a long while; for example, what to do upon graduating from college. Others are thrust upon us suddenly: an unexpected offer to take on a major commitment at church. Yet others can brew or stew slowly over time, such as a growing sense of disillusionment and frustration with our current job.

Situations like these ultimately demand some kind of decision. Assuming we seek to honor God in all areas of our lives—our marriages and families, other personal relationships, career preparation, the workplace, our church lives—we are concerned to make a godly choice. But how? Clearly, guidance *is* a difficult area for Christians.

God guides those who genuinely seek His will, and He desires only the best for His children.

The fact that scores of books on the topic have appeared over the past several decades testifies to the ongoing quest for counsel on this front. This book is intended to assist you in thinking through questions about guidance more incisively and, if you heed the shared wisdom on this topic as handed down from 2,000 years of our faith, help you make wiser, more thoughtful, and more godly choices. The generalizations presented here are distilled from the wisdom of numerous thoughtful writers on this topic. In essence, the thoughts in this book are not new. The hope is, however, that their presentation and format will make these ideas more accessible and easier to understand and apply in your life.

It's plain that Christians could use ongoing help in this area. "In our quest for God's guidance," said J. I. Packer, the British theologian and scholar, "we become our own worst enemies, and our mistakes attest to our nuttiness in this area." This book is an attempt to head off some of those self-defeating tendencies and minimize the nuttiness. In doing so, this book differs from other writings on guidance in two ways. The first is its emphasis. This volume assumes what other authors carefully and painstakingly identify: the ample scriptural evidence that God guides those who genuinely seek His will, and that He desires only the best for His children. So, the assumption here is that you don't need to be persuaded that God is both able and eager to guide us.

The second difference lies in this book's approach. The typical book on guidance offers systematic, chapter-length expositions on the nature of guidance and its relationship to vital Christian living. By contrast, the approach here is far more hands-on, identifying practical problem areas, possible stumbling blocks, areas of confusion, and any other aspects of guidance that can lead to the mistakes and nuttiness to which Packer refers. What follows is a series of thoughts on topics about guidance. Each topic, summarized as a principle or key concept, serves as a stepping stone through what can often be a mental and spiritual swamp for Christians who earnestly seek God's will and direction, but who have learned that discovering it isn't easy or necessarily clear cut.

All the topics are built around a foundational section called "The Big Five—and Beyond." This is the assumption repeated by many writers that guidance is normally the product of five elements. They are:

1. A careful reliance on Scriptures
2. Prayer
3. The advice of mature Christians
4. A consideration of our circumstances
5. A sense of inner peace

It is typically the combination of these five ingredients that helps lead us toward sound, godly decisions.

Something else that holds together the 62 principles in this book is the understanding that guidance is a process that involves carefully thinking through and incorporating "The Big Five," as well as other issues pertinent to your situation. At the end of this Introduction is a set of common questions about guidance, along with the topics that are likely to help you most with each question. **Please read "The Big Five—and Beyond" before dipping into other topics.** Without the context it provides, the other sections will be less helpful than you would like. A note on footnotes: for the most part, I've tried to avoid cluttering your reading and limited footnotes to some lesser known authors on whom you may want to know the source.

The 62 topics, and the principles on which they are based, are presented as generalizations. And because we know every generalization is false (including this one), one needs to see them as part of the broader whole. Nor are these principles necessarily to be read in order. After reading **The Big Five [1]**, feel free to browse and pick and choose among the topics that most interest you. Many of the topics contain cross-references to other parts of the book, using the section number so that you can easily find what you're looking for.

Some Underlying Assumptions

As you read the pages ahead, please be aware of the following assumptions that underlie and are woven through the 62 principles. This book assumes that:

1. You take your Christian commitment seriously and, above everything else, seek to live a God-pleasing life. In other words, you earnestly seek God's will for your life, not His seal of approval for what you plan to do anyway.
2. You take the authority of Scripture seriously and are willing to apply its guidelines to all areas of your life.
3. You already are convinced that God is able and willing to guide you in all aspects of your walk with Him, and accept that He will do so on His terms and with His timing.
4. You take seriously your God-given ability to think through whatever guidance issues you face.

It's important to note a truly astonishing reality. We claim as part of the Christian faith that not only did the Lord of the universe send His Son to die for us and redeem us from our sins, but that His interest and love for us continues day by day. Like the most loving of parents, God Himself seeks to guide and direct every facet of our lives.

Two reality checks also need mentioning. The first is that living our lives in a God-directed manner is never easy. Living as we do with our sinful natures and an always-present vulnerability to temptation, it is extremely difficult to do what we know we should, and avoid what we know we shouldn't. Paul said, "I do not understand what I do. For what I want to do I do not do, but what I hate to do" (Romans 7:15). If living the day-by-day dimension of the Christian life is difficult, it's no easier when we face those extraordinary moments, the times when tough choices must be made. Søren Kierkegaard, the nineteenth-century Danish philosopher and theologian, said: "It is perfectly true, as philosophers say, that life must be understood backwards. But . . . it must be lived forwards."

As we grapple with trying to understand God's guidance in our lives, we often recognize His leading only as we look back. But we must make difficult choices while living life in forward mode. No book on guidance can completely answer anyone's questions; we each need to answer those ourselves. This book, in other words, cannot provide simple, formulaic answers to the deep needs you have for guidance. The ideas outlined here are only tools, and apart from your deep commitment to seeking God's will and your willingness to struggle through issues, they are worthless. You will be disappointed if you're hoping this collection of ideas will tell you whether God wants you to attend college X or take that job in Cleveland. That is for you to work out. All this book can do is help you in that process.

Another reality worth noting concerns our limitations in understanding how God moves in our lives. It is the height of presumption to think that any book can prescribe how God may choose to reveal Himself to any of us. The only absolute we can be sure of in this regard is that God will not guide us in a way that is contrary to what He has already revealed to us about His nature.

A final thought on "God's perfect plan for our lives." While Christians agree that God is keenly interested in our lives, they differ on the degree to which He has a "perfect plan" mapped out for each of us. Some contend that God has a carefully worked out blueprint for our lives: His guidance helps us discover that perfect will, and His Holy Spirit helps us live it out. Other Christians see this approach as artificially narrow. God, they believe, is not boxed into some lockstep, foreordained approach to how our lives unfold. God's grace, power, and imagination surely transcend whatever mistakes we make or sins we commit, which would presumably otherwise doom us to live by a "second best" plan. Rather, God is always able to take the lives of those committed to Him, regardless of how far we might have fallen from His standards in the past, and offer the constant, uninhibited love and direction that He promises His people.

If the issue of a "perfect plan" is important to you, you should know that the bias of this book is clearly toward the latter position. God's boundless grace in His dealings with us makes Him love us no less when we choose something other than His best at any given moment. Yes, God's discipline may follow our poor choices. But for the Christian who is wholeheartedly seeking God's will, He presents us with far more of a buffet table of legitimate options and choices than some stiflingly healthy yet tasteless diet. A. W. Tozer said, "The man or woman who is wholly or joyously surrendered to Christ can't make a wrong choice—any choice will be the right one."

That remark captures much of the spirit with which this book is written: that ours is a God of freedom, whose guidance we can seek with confidence and enthusiasm. He's a God of infinite love who enthusiastically champions our case and seeks our best. He is the architect wanting to help us build holy lives, lived to the full (John 10:10). Yet we sometimes regard Him as the county planning officer who's looking for every weakness in our plans, smugly catching yet another way we've fallen short of the building code. God is not a stickler; rather, He's the architect who brings our possibilities to reality for our benefit and for His pleasure.

This book is an attempt to help you along as you invite God, the ultimate architect, to help you build your life in keeping with His overall design to make us holy persons. From the foundations to the finishing touches, He is there and eager to help at each step. The pages that follow are intended to help you build your own house of faith that shall last through eternity.

Don't be a spiritual Lone Ranger;

when you think you see God's will, have your per-

ception checked. Draw on the wisdom of those

who are wiser than you are. Take advice.

J. I. Packer

Approaching Guidance Issues

This is the confidence
we have in
approaching God:
that if we ask
anything
according to
his will,
he hears us.

1 John 5:14

1 The Big Five — and Beyond

Every quest for guidance should be shaped by scriptural guidelines, prayer, the advice of other Christians, the circumstances we face, and an overall sense that this course is what God wants.

It's the big picture that counts. A recurring theme found in books on guidance is that you need to look at this big picture as a whole when making major decisions concerning God's will. Far from basing our decision entirely on a chance remark made in last Sunday's sermon, or on an obscure verse in 2 Kings, God expects us to use all the vehicles He's made available for our decision making. That's why it's important to consider *each* of The Big Five factors listed here and see how they mesh together as we consider our decision. Again, these five factors are:

- Scriptural guidelines
- Prayer
- The advice of other Christians
- The circumstances we face
- A sense of inner peace about our decision

How Guidance Works

I don't doubt that the Holy Spirit guides your decisions from within when you make them with the intention of pleasing God. The error would be to think that he speaks *only* within, whereas in reality he speaks also through Scripture, the church, Christian friends, books, etc.

—C. S. Lewis

Until you've got a "thumbs up" on each of the five, you're probably not ready to make a decision. If, for example, you're seriously thinking of leaving your job to go to seminary but your closest friends are advising you against it, you need to check your thinking. Or if you've been invited to go on a short-term mission trip and the first four points check out just fine, yet you've still got a nagging feeling that something isn't right, once again it may be best to hold off on your decision.

If you were leaving later today for a trip abroad, you'd make sure you'd taken care of your passport, air ticket, health insurance, luggage, and spending money. If you were heading for the airport and realized you'd left your passport at home, it's unlikely you would keep going and say, "Well, four out of five isn't bad."

Similarly, you're probably asking for trouble by heading into a decision without a check mark against each of The Big Five. Is it possible that your friends' advice is wrong? Or that you're confusing a lack of inner peace about a decision with plain old nervousness? Of course. The point here isn't that missing one of these five checkpoints means you shouldn't go ahead; it simply means there's a warning light on the dashboard and you're well advised to take a second look at what's happening. Or, to switch metaphors, if these five principles don't line up neatly like lights on a runway, you need to question seriously whether you're ready to come in for a landing.

Sometimes those landing lights don't line up neatly, or one warning light keeps flickering on the dash—and a major decision still looms. Remember, guidance is seldom a simple, clear-cut process. Because working toward the decisions God would have us make can be complex, sometimes with ambiguous answers, it's necessary to dig deeper in our understanding of The Big Five.

The separate entries of The Big Five are not of equal importance. The simple flowchart that follows shows that scriptural principles are the starting point.

But they're *only* the starting point. *Each* of these five principles merits careful attention. The next step is to examine any of these five elements that merits special attention in your situation: **Scripture [2], Prayer [3], Advice [4], Circumstances [5],** or **Inner Peace [6].** Alternatively, you may want to turn directly to other individual topics that speak to your needs. The Guidance Road Map on page 13 will help you do that. Or you may simply want to browse.

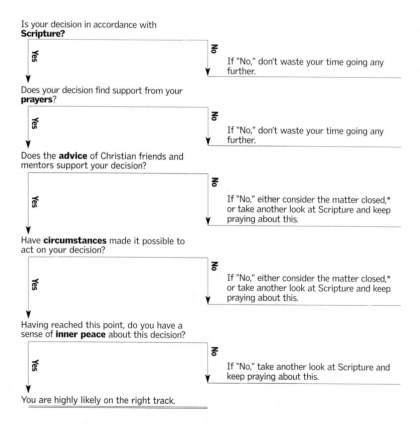

Is your decision in accordance with
Scripture?

Yes ↓   No →   If "No," don't waste your time going any
                        further.

Does your decision find support from your
prayers?

Yes ↓   No →   If "No," don't waste your time going any
                        further.

Does the **advice** of Christian friends and
mentors support your decision?

Yes ↓   No →   If "No," either consider the matter closed,*
                        or take another look at Scripture and keep
                        praying about this.

Have **circumstances** made it possible to
act on your decision?

Yes ↓   No →   If "No," either consider the matter closed,*
                        or take another look at Scripture and keep
                        praying about this.

Having reached this point, do you have a
sense of **inner peace** about this decision?

Yes ↓   No →   If "No," take another look at Scripture and
                        keep praying about this.

You are highly likely on the right track.

Or perhaps you need to consider a similar decision, starting again at the top of the chart.

2 Scripture

Scripture is a foundational and sufficient basis for the general principles of Christian living; for the particulars of our daily lives we may need to supplement its directions with the other elements in **The Big Five [1].**

Scripture — What Is It Good For?

All Scripture is inspired by God and can profitably be used for teaching, for refuting error, for guiding people's lives and teaching them to be holy.

—2 Timothy 3:16 (JB)

More than any other avenue, God is likely to use Scripture to light our way. Especially when it comes to the general principles that should mark our Christian lives, Scripture is a complete, coherent, and trustworthy guide. We know that we can trust Scripture to give us all we need to know about God's general will. But as Paul emphasizes in 2 Timothy, Scripture is not only reliable, it's intensely practical and applicable to our lives. It is both authoritative and useful. This quality of "usefulness" is of central importance to our daily lives as Christians and takes on a special relevance when we're dealing with guidance issues.

The Bible thus identifies the general principles that will point us to the ultimate meaning and purpose of our lives (to be holy and become more like Christ) and, more practically, will convey what kind of husband or wife we should seek and be, or what kind of employer or employee to be. But the Bible will not, and cannot, be comparably helpful in showing us God's specific will. (See **God's Will [25].**)

At the specific level where we often seek answers, when we want to know whether to marry person X or Y, Scripture will typically be of limited help. The reason, as indicated in **Clear Thinking [9]** and **Do What You Like [31],** is that after showing us the general principles God wants us to follow, He gives us considerable freedom in making choices that are pleasing to Him.

Yet the Bible must always be our starting point in the guidance process. Hannah Whitall Smith puts it well when she writes, "The Scriptures come first. If you are in doubt upon any subject, you must, first of all, consult the Bible about it, and see whether there is any law there to direct you. Until you have found and obeyed God's will as it is there revealed, you must not ask nor expect a separate, direct, personal revelation."[1] If Scripture has spoken clearly on some issue, we ought not to keep looking for alternative answers. For example, if we're seriously thinking of marrying someone who isn't a Christian, we don't need any more guidance than what God has plainly told us in 2 Corinthians 6:14: "Do not be yoked together with unbelievers."

At times God will speak to us in our specific situations through a particular Bible passage. Most often, though, we do Scripture an injustice if we expect detailed guidance from it. We wouldn't turn to the Sermon on the Mount for instructions on repairing a toaster. Likewise, we shouldn't demand detailed solutions from Scripture to our guidance needs that simply aren't there. Max Anders notes that the "Bible does not give us a road map for life, but it does give us a compass."[2]

We must study Scripture regularly, for two reasons. The first is to have a high level of understanding of God's overall purposes for our lives, so that when guidance issues arise we will already know the rules of the game. G. Campbell Morgan says, "We are regularly, and devotionally, and intelligently, to study [Scripture], in order that we may discover the revelation of principles. Where this is done as a habit of the life, the mind will act under the power of these principles."[3] (See **Getting Ready for Guidance [24].**)

The second reason to study Scripture is for those moments of special need, when we must remind ourselves of Scripture's basic truths and open ourselves to any special leading from the Holy Spirit as we immerse ourselves in Scripture and prayer.

The principles that Scripture provides are all we need to point us in the right direction and to keep us on the right track. When we need those "road map" details for guidance, we look to the other elements in **The Big Five [1]** to fill out the picture. But our conclusions about where God is leading us must always arise from and remain rooted in what we learn from Scripture.

However, we should not treat Scripture like a collection of fortune cookie solutions to our guidance needs, thinking we can meet them with the easy, one-step finger-pointing technique. The classic example of the dangers of this approach is demonstrated by a man who wanted to know God's will for his life. Flipping open the Bible and pointing randomly to a verse, he came up with: "Then [Judas] went away and hanged himself"

(Matthew 27:5). Convinced that wasn't quite what God had in mind for him, he tried the finger jabbing approach again, landing on Luke 10:37: "Go and do likewise." Shaken, he tried one more time—and got John 13:27: "What you are about to do, do quickly." Of course, that's not a true story. But it's about the quality of guidance you can expect with the finger-pointing approach. Worse, though, is the disrespect we show God and His Word in the process when we take the richness of Scripture and reduce it to some kind of magical crystal ball. Bruce Waltke says that "The use of promise boxes, or flipping your Bible open and pointing your finger, or relying on the first thought to enter your mind after a prayer are unwarranted forms of Christian divination."[4]

A related but different danger is taking verses out of the context of a fuller understanding of Scripture. Hannah Whitall Smith tells of an "earnest Christian woman who had the text 'All things are yours' [1 Corinthians 3:21] so strongly impressed upon her mind in reference to some money belonging to a friend, that she felt it was a direct command to her to steal that money," which she did.[5] But if she'd only evaluated what she thought was her "leading" in the light of overall biblical teaching, Smith says, she wouldn't have ended up in the trouble she did. This is a glaring example of how not to use Scripture. All of us, though, may at times be tempted to use Scripture for our own ends. (See **Mixed Motives [54].**)

The Basics of Understanding the Bible

This is not the place to discuss at length any detailed principles on how to read and interpret Scripture. Seminarians spend several years training to do that. But it's important to remind ourselves of some basic principles of understanding the Bible, especially as it affects our questions on guidance.

- Interpret passages or books of Scripture according to the form of expression in which they were written (that is, don't take poetry literally, or a parable as a historical story).
- Try to learn the meaning of the original text.
- Try to learn what the text would have meant to its original readers.
- Interpret Scripture in the light of what the rest of Scripture says. (See the example

above on the danger of prooftexting—stringing together an inappropriate series of Bible verses to prove one's theology.)

- Recognize the overall purpose of Scripture, which is to describe how God deals with human beings, their need for salvation, and how through Christ this is made possible.
- Regard Christ as the central theme of both the Old and New Testaments.
- Interpret Scripture with common sense, taking words and sentences in their contexts. (Remember, just because Satan's words appear in the Bible doesn't make him any more trustworthy!)

In the end, any reading *about* Scripture such as you're doing here never substitutes for knowing God's Word directly as you seek His guidance. With fullest confidence we can join in the psalmist's prayer, "give me understanding according to your word" (Psalm 119:169).

3 Prayer

Like the other elements in The Big Five, prayer is crucial, but by itself is not a sufficient ingredient for knowing God's will.

Prayer is indispensable for discovering God's will and to obtain the wisdom and grace we need to live it out. Scripture offers us abundant guidance on God's general will for our lives and we don't need to spend much (or any) time in prayer figuring that out. Still, Christians must turn to prayer for two needs: to discover God's particular will for our lives, and for the

Resources on Guidance from Scripture

If you'd like more help in the area of guidance from Scripture, you can turn to any of a number of good books. Four popular titles are:

30 *Days to Understanding the Bible* by Max Anders

How to Study Your Bible by Kay Arthur

How to Read the Bible for All Its Worth by Gordon D. Fee and Douglas Stuart

Living by the Book by Howard D. Hendricks and William D. Hendricks

See also **Key Scripture Verses [60].**

Praying with Perspective

When we pray it is far more important to pray with a sense of the greatness of God than with a sense of the greatness of the problem.

—Evangeline Blood

empowerment to live out what we know to do.

Over the past 2,000 years, Christian writers have built a massive treasury of literature on prayer. Rather than attempting to summarize this material, this section can best speak to your interest in guidance by pointing to several places where prayer and guidance overlap. The following eight points are worth considering.

1. We are to take prayer seriously.

Jesus' example makes plain that His disciples must take seriously the need to pray. Not only did Jesus model this for us, but His words indicated an assumption that prayer is an integral ingredient in the life of God's people. For example, He said several times in the Sermon on the Mount, *"when* you pray . . . "* (Matthew 6:5-7, emphasis added). Later in that chapter, when He gives us the Lord's Prayer, He says "This, then, is how you should pray . . . " His warning against attention-getting, empty, or repetitious prayers in these three verses offers a sharp contrast to the sincerity and genuineness God expects in our prayers. In the words of H. E. Fosdick, we are to avoid the tendency to make our prayers *"a pious form* and not a *vital transaction."* We are to approach God in prayer with a seriousness befitting the One to whom it is addressed.

In addition, if the only time we come to God in prayer is when we have a need for guidance, we have a prayer life in need of a tune-up. God welcomes and wants our petitions, yet if He hears from us only in times of trouble and need, we act like the self-absorbed teenager who speaks to his mom or dad only when he needs the car or his allowance. However loving his parents may be, and however generous their hearts, their son's "gimme" attitude must sadden them greatly. With God our prayer life should be far richer—characterized also by prayers of adoration, confession, thanksgiving, and requests on behalf of others. Yes, God eagerly seeks to meet our needs too, but if we present those needs only in a context of spiritual self-absorption, we have more than matters of guidance that God would like us to deal with.

2. We are to pray with expectancy that God will guide us.

Scripture is replete with encouragements for us to bring our needs before God, confident that He will both hear and answer. In Matthew 7:7, for instance, Jesus gave us these familiar words: "Ask and it will be given to you; seek and you will find; knock and the door will be opened to you."

> *"But when he, the Spirit of truth, comes, he will guide you into all truth."*
> —John 16:13

3. We are to pray with an openness to hearing and doing God's will.

As the section on **God's Will [25]**, among others, makes clear, we ought to approach God with sincere openness to whatever He may wish to tell us. It's no coincidence that in His model prayer, Jesus gave us the words, "Your kingdom come, your will be done." Thus, the emphasis in our prayers is always to be on *God's* will, not ours. In addition, the various preconditions that we need to meet for receiving guidance apply equally well to how we approach God in prayer. (See **Conditional Guidance [21]**.)

4. We are to pray with patience.

Jesus demonstrated in the parable in Luke 18:1-8 that if even an unjust judge will finally do the right thing in response to persistent requests, we can be fully confident that a loving God will hear our prayers and answer them. Patience doesn't come easily; **Waiting [40]** simply isn't something we mortals are naturally inclined to do well.

5. We are to pray knowing that our understanding of our requests may be extremely limited.

When we don't get the answers we expect, the explanation may lie in what we've asked. Given our partial understand of God's purposes, even when we genuinely seek His will in our prayers we can never fully grasp what His overarching, eternal purposes might be. An example involves St. Augustine, one of the giants in the history of the church. He lived a profligate, wild youth in his North African home, despite his Christian mother's prayers for his conversion. When he planned to take off for Italy, her prayers intensified, as she feared that away from home and her

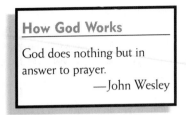

How God Works

God does nothing but in answer to prayer.
—John Wesley

influence he would be even less likely to come to Christ. Yet her prayers were unanswered, and he went to Milan—which is where he met the famous Bishop Ambrose, was converted, and became one of the church's greatest theologians. His mother's specific prayer was not answered, but the desire behind it was. Her limited knowledge of how God worked understandably shaped her pleas, but her faith was ultimately honored in ways she would never have predicted.

6. We need to know when we ought to move from prayer to action.

Sometimes praying to know God's will simply isn't necessary. Maybe we're dealing with an issue to which we already know the answer—or at least enough of the answer to act now. For instance, if we've been laid off from work, we should certainly be praying that God will lead us to discover what He wants us to do next. But we can, and should, in the meantime be working on a job-hunting strategy and updating our resumes; God won't miraculously do that for us. And we need to hit the phones to do some networking, check the want ads, or do whatever is appropriate in our situation, energetically taking on what we already know to do. As Jeremy Taylor wrote in the seventeenth century, "Whatsoever we beg of God, let us also work for it." While we may not know what job He has lined up for us next, we should be hard at work looking for it. Praying without also doing will probably lead to a disappointing outcome. If we begin tackling those parts of God's will that we already know to do, and keep praying for direction on the parts that remain a mystery to us, He will let us know what our next steps are in His good time.

7. We need to pray with an expectation of surprises, and an openness to possibly unwelcome answers.

We know that God sometimes gives us answers that we don't expect, or, if we're honest, we would rather not have received at all. Prayer, after all, is what G. Christie Swain describes as "dangerous business."[6] Or, in the words of Geoffrey Chaucer, "We little know the things for which we pray." Should the answers to our prayers take us by surprise, we might well find our **Obedience [57]** put to the test. As the section on **Conditional Guidance [21]** makes plain, if we are to optimize our chances of discerning God's leading in the first place, we need to be committed in advance to honoring whatever the answers to our prayers might be.

> *"And if you have faith, everything you ask for in prayer, you will receive."*
> —Matthew 21:22 (JB)

8. We are not to be sidetracked by some of the questions raised about prayer.

Two common questions arise concerning prayers for guidance. One is, Why should we pray for guidance in the first place? Aren't we telling God what He already knows to be our needs? The other is, How can we be sure that what we think are answers to prayer are God's voice, not our own? Each merits a brief response.

Those raising the first issue perhaps assume that while God knows our needs, He won't meet them until we come before Him in begging mode. Only with appropriate servility on our part, goes this thinking, will God respond. But this depiction of God flies completely in the face of what we know to be His tender, parental character, as outlined in **The "Abba, Father" Principle [18]**. Far from meeting our needs only grudgingly, He is even more ready to give than we are to receive.

Another problem with the idea that there is no need for us to pray is the implication that we are not needed in accomplishing God's purposes. Not so, says H. E. Fosdick, who says there are "some things [that] God never can do until He finds a man who prays." He continues: "We pray for the same reason that we work and think, because only so can the wise and good God get some things done which He wants done." Fosdick rightly emphasizes the extraordinary truth that God invites us to be His collaborators in accomplishing His purposes. Richard Foster expresses this idea when he observes that "We are working with God to

> ### Digging Deeper
>
> Ron Kincaid's book, *Praying for Guidance: How to Discover God's Will*, offers a thoughtful set of ideas and insights on prayer's role in guidance.

determine the future! Certain things will happen in history if we pray rightly. We are to change the world by prayer." Far from being expected to accept passively and fatalistically whatever God has decreed, He invites us to help shape His kingdom—through our prayers, thinking, and actions.

Think About It

In addition to your own prayers for guidance and those found in **Prayers [61]**, consider praying some of the Scripture verses previously listed and in **Key Scripture Verses [60]**.

The second common concern that is identified asks whether it's *God's* voice we're hearing and not simply our own thoughts. This legitimate issue is addressed more fully in **Listening [13]**, but for now the assurance of John White is sufficient: "If I but concern myself with hearing the voice of the Shepherd, paying heed to Christ, obeying him, doing his will, I shall find that the problem of distinguishing his voice will begin to take care of itself."

By itself, prayer is an inadequate vehicle for knowing what God wants us to do. Apart from a sound understanding of what the Bible says about God's general will, prayer by itself is of limited value. We know God will never answer our prayers in a way that contradicts what He's told us in **Scripture [2]**. Therefore, the Bible needs to be the touchstone by which we evaluate what we think might be God's answers to our prayers. Here is not the place to describe the benefits of what Richard Foster describes as "the discipline of prayer." He and many other writers point to the need for and value of deep, meditative prayer. But our prayers need to be grounded in a biblical understanding of God's character, His general will, and His specific will for us, if they are to yield answers on which we can act with confidence.

4 Advice

Always seek the advice of mature Christians to affirm and confirm what you think God is telling you.

Seeking advice from other Christians on a question of guidance is a sign of strength, not weakness. Proverbs 13:10 says, "[W]isdom is found in those who take

Advise Yourself

Before seeking help from anyone else, imagine that you've come to yourself for advice. What would you tell yourself? It may be that the answers are so clear and simple that you don't need any extra input.

advice." It is a mark of maturity, not shallowness, in our Christian faith. Like each of **The Big Five [1],** the need for advice is an invaluable element in the guidance process for several reasons.

The first reason is that God says so. The book of Proverbs is explicit about the need to seek out wise counselors who can steer us in a godly direction. For example, Proverbs 12:15 says, "The way of a fool seems right to him, but a wise man listens to advice." In addition, a handful of other practical reasons make advice-seeking necessary. We're limited in our own knowledge and judgment, and others who care about us may stretch our perspectives on the options we face, or point out pitfalls we haven't considered. Sometimes we're timid or unsure about pursuing a certain course and good advice can be as much an encouragement as it can be a confirmation we're on the right track. Or we may have an opposite need: to temper unwarranted enthusiasm and require us to think twice about a step we're planning to take.

Do You Really Need Advice?

Not all advice is helpful, or even necessary. Before stepping out to seek help, the following pointers may clarify your thinking.

- Ask if this is a matter on which you, in fact, need any advice. If you face a clear-cut issue that Scripture gives plain guidelines on, you don't need advice on decision-making. For example, you may feel guilty about being in an extremely damaging relationship and are considering breaking it off. If so, you probably don't need any advice on whether to do that; that may already be obvious. It may simply be that you need encouragement and support as you take a necessary but difficult step.

- Choose your advisors carefully. Scripture cautions us to seek advice from godly persons, and that to do otherwise is courting disaster. Turn only to those whose Christian maturity and judgment you trust. (And those who can be trusted to keep quiet, if necessary.)

- Seek out only those who you believe would care enough about you to give honest, and possibly unwelcome, advice. You may not realize it, but you may be seeking reinforcement for what you've already decided to do. If so, then you're really seeking cheerleaders rather than advisors. If you're genuinely open to how God might use people to shape your thinking, listen to them carefully, especially if the advice isn't what you want or expect.

- Ask whether you're seeking advice to discern God's leading or whether you may be doing what Dudley Delffs warns against in *Seeking God's Will*: "Perhaps we're even looking for answers from others because it's a lot easier than waiting for God to direct us."

- Choose only a few confidants on the issue at hand. It's helpful to seek a variety of perspectives, but no more than five or six individuals. If you talk to sixty rather than six, you're conducting an opinion poll rather than seeking personal advice.

- Be prepared for conflicting advice. Even thoughtful, godly people may differ widely in their opinions on what you should do. Don't be discouraged or confused by seemingly contradictory advice. Be willing to work through the issues and options they raise, while at the same time remaining committed not simply to seek "advice" that echoes what you've already quietly decided to do.

Remember, no matter how good the advice you receive, the decision you face is still *yours*. It is *you*, together with God's help, who need to decide. Don't look to others to make a decision on your behalf, or worse still, see them as possible scapegoats if the decision goes bad. It's your decision, and you need to take full responsibility for it. Indeed, beware of anyone who wants to make a decision for you. G. Campbell Morgan writes that "No Spirit-taught man or woman will pretend to be able to decide for a second person."[7] See also **Formation Flying [35].**

5 Circumstances

While never the final word, circumstances can help us sort through the authentic and unreliable messages we may get in the guidance process.

> ## Circumstances That Fit
>
> When we are acting in line with God's will, surrounding circumstances will fall out accordingly.
> —J. Oswald Sanders

Guidance always needs to be responded to in some context—that of our education, our personal lives, our careers, our church lives, and so on. That context is made up of constantly changing circumstances that make a step we're considering possible or impossible, wise or unwise. The challenge we face is knowing how to "read" the road map of circumstances presented to us at any given time.

One danger is to accept our circumstances fatalistically, unquestioningly accepting whatever situation we find ourselves in. If we should be making some changes, resigning ourselves to our circumstances could mean giving up in the face of the slightest barriers we encounter. Alternatively, if our tendency is toward inertia, God may have a harder time getting our attention if He wants to move us beyond our present comfort zone to a new place in His kingdom. As we consider our circumstances, they can so preoccupy us that we read far more into ordinary, routine events than is healthy or sane. Every little development may lead us to lurch one way and then another in our thinking, convinced that God is now calling us to do this or that.

The way around these dangers is to assign circumstances their proper role in the guidance process. That role is a secondary one, and must always be subject to our overall understanding of God's general will for our lives, as we know it from **Scripture [2]**. (See **God's Will [25]**.) If, and only if, the circumstances in which we find ourselves are fitting into that bigger picture can we begin to look seriously at what they may mean.

Circumstances are closely linked to **Doors—Open and Closed [10]**. Just because things may appear favorable, it doesn't mean a possible path is necessarily the correct one. Seemingly favorable circumstances can be deceiving.

What Would Jonah Do?

Consider Jonah. We all know how he decided against going to Nineveh, for reasons of his own, and concluded he'd rather head in the opposite direction—to Tarshish. That community could also use a prophetic word from God, couldn't they? Then, showing up in Joppa, he finds a ship heading just that direction. The odds of a ship going his way exactly when he wanted it were slim, so this development must surely be God's way of affirming Jonah's new direction.

Bruce Dunn says that Jonah may well have asked himself, "Who can arrange timing like this but God?" Dunn adds: "The only problem was that his circumstances contradicted what God had told him. He'd already been told where he was to go and what he was to do. It's easy sometimes to think because things are going well, we're in the center of God's will."[8] The lesson is clear: When things are going well, they may well reflect that we're doing what God wants, but that's not necessarily the case. We should constantly examine the motives behind our quest for guidance. In addition, we should also test the circumstances we face and see how they fit into **The Big Five [1]** as a whole.

Similarly, when things are not coming together as we might hope, it doesn't mean we should give up trying to pursue what we think God wants of us. It may be that we need to wait longer for God to work out His purposes, or that we're simply facing tough times even though we're doing exactly what God wants us to do. (See **When Guidance "Goes Wrong" [59].**)

We can be sure that as we work our way through the guidance process, our circumstances will eventually line up. Even though our circumstances may be the last piece of the guidance puzzle that falls into place, we can be confident that because God is sovereign over every aspect of our lives, He will make possible what He wants to happen to and for us. J. Oswald Sanders writes in *Every Life a Plan of God*: "When circumstances are in keeping with the tenor of Scripture, and coincide with the informed judgment of the believer and the inner conviction of the Holy Spirit, then they serve as a confirmation of the choice made."

Our circumstances are never to be taken as the final word in guidance; they must always be part of the overall process. Especially when we're dealing with major decisions, it's a good rule of thumb to ensure that our circumstances play a secondary role in guidance. They should confirm whatever else we've learned through Scripture, prayer, and our own judgment about

> ### The Place of Circumstances
>
> Do not put circumstances above God's Word. Don't allow circumstances to contradict God's Word.
> —Bruce Waltke[9]

the direction we should go. In other words, they should affirm, not dictate, what we understand to be God's leading in our lives.

See also **Clear Thinking [9]; Signs and Wonders [39].**

6 Inner Peace

Inner peace is necessary. But by itself it's not a sufficient condition for choosing a course of action.

Inner peace should be the culmination of the guidance process. If we've worked our way carefully through each of the previous four steps in **The Big Five [1]**, then this stage presents a final checkpoint. We're talking here about a sense of "rightness" of our decision or our choice "making sense" in the light of the Scripture reading and praying we've done. Moreover, the decision or choice that lies ahead of us seems also to be compatible with both the advice we've received and the circumstances we face. If all of this is in place, then we come to the point where we ask, "Does all of this come together in a way that makes me confident God is wanting me to move ahead?" Then we can trust the Holy Spirit to give us a sense of well being and correctness about the next step—or, conversely, that the Holy Spirit will leave us unsettled or uncomfortable about going ahead if we ought not to.

It's important to mention here that what we should feel comfortable about is the *decision* or *choice* that lies ahead. The sense of inner peace needs to be about the correctness of this step itself; it is *not* about the implications of that step.

Two Examples: One Pleasant, One Not

EXAMPLE ONE: If you have concluded that God is calling you to ask Camilla to marry you, you should certainly sense God's peace over that decision. Of course, actually asking her could be marked by nervousness, apprehension, or worse — nothing that resembles anything that you'd call inner peace. Also, there may be significant barriers you'll have to deal with if she says yes (a lack of money, opposition from her family or yours, and so on). The ripples of your decision may be far from comforting or peaceful.

EXAMPLE TWO: You're a manager who's decided to fire an employee. You are clear, after working through the guidance process carefully, that this is the right, although difficult, thing to do. While you have a sense of inner peace about what to do, you are likely to feel far from peaceful about the implications of dismissing someone, as you think of the impact on that employee and his or her family. Beware of confusing the consequences of your action, unsettling though they may be for you, with the rightness of the decision.

We need to be clear that we desire a sense of calm and assurance about the *decision itself* for which we have sought guidance. Actually implementing that decision may call for considerable **Courage [47]** and a special measure of God's grace. Nowhere in Scripture are we assured that living out God's will is going to be easy or comfortable. For example, the call of Samuel as a young boy left him with no doubt that God Himself required him to deliver a message to the priest Eli. The boy presumably had inner peace about needing to take the next step. He surely did not relish having to convey to his mentor the damning news: "The guilt of Eli's house will never be atoned for by sacrifice or offering" (1 Samuel 3:14). On that point he presumably had little inner peace, as he had to act with a holy impertinence toward the aged priest.

Having a sense of inner peace about a decision is meaningless, though, if it stands by itself; without the presence of the other elements of The Big Five, feeling okay about a decision tells us nothing. Even if we've worked our way carefully through the entire guidance process, this final test is the least reliable of The Big Five. It's far more subjective than the other four, and is therefore far more prone to being influenced by our wants and motives. Because of our limitations as sinful individuals, it's extremely difficult to know with absolute certainty that we're making a choice that God wants us to. It's prudent, therefore, to be cautious in our reliance on our sense of inner peace about a choice or decision. Humility demands that, even if we feel assured we're on the right track, we move forward surrounding our decision in prayer that God will still stop us if we're wrong.

What if we don't have such a sense of peace? Any doubts or misgivings should be looked at particularly carefully. If the doubts are substantial, then it's not time to move ahead. But what if we're facing a quiet, almost inaudible nagging? Could that simply be nervousness? Yes. It could also be an important warning signal to pause and dig deeper in our thinking and praying before we move on. It could be that we're simply facing a case of nerves about the implications of what lies ahead, and not about the decision itself. Clarifying that distinction may give us the answer we need. Whatever the outcome, moving ahead without this inner peace is never wise. An absence of warning signals may not absolutely guarantee that we're doing the right thing, but ignoring any we do hear is surely an invitation to trouble.

See also **Doubts [48]; Intuition and Feelings [12].**

Knowing His Will

I am satisfied that when the Almighty wants me to do or not to do any particular thing, he finds a way of letting me know it.

Abraham Lincoln

*If any of you lacks
wisdom, he should ask
God, who gives
generously to all
without finding fault,
and it will be
given to him.*

James 1:15

7 Asking the Right Questions

Work on asking the right questions; avoid those that are already settled, pointless, or irrelevant.

Management consultant Peter Drucker has said nothing is as pointless as working hard on the wrong priorities. Similarly, in seeking God's answers for our situation, we ought to concentrate on asking the most meaningful and helpful questions. If we seek God's answers, we should also be aware of God's questions. What is important to *Him* as we make our decisions?

Here's a list to help your thinking. Not all will apply equally well (or even at all) in your circumstances. But some will help you evaluate a decision you're thinking of making.

- Is this decision likely to honor God and reflect well on His kingdom?
- Can I justify my decision to other Christians? To God?
- If anyone is likely to disagree with my decision, or be hurt by it, on what biblical basis can I defend this decision?
- Is this decision conducive to my spiritual growth?
- Does this decision match the kind of Christian life I wish to live?

- If I think ahead five years, how am I likely to look back on this decision?
- Have I given this decision the prayer, time, and reflection it deserves?
- What would Jesus do in my situation? (If applicable, answer this question to the best of your ability.)

See also **Testing, Testing [16]; Trivial Pursuit [27]; What Would Jesus Do? [41].**

8 Change

Change is at the heart of guidance. God brings us to a point where we must embrace or resist a new step in our lives. If you're uncomfortable about change, prepare for what could be a rough ride.

Change is an integral part of guidance. After all, we speak of praying for God's *leading*, for His showing us what should be the next step in our walk with Him. Even if He shows us that He wants us to do nothing and mark time, the prospect of change is inherent in all guidance. The changes we face can be divided into three

> **Change Lasts**
>
> There is nothing permanent except change.
>
> —Heraclitus

broad categories: the fully expected, the complete surprises, and those that come upon us more slowly.

Several biblical examples illustrate the first two types. Joshua 1 describes the long-awaited changes that Moses' successor faced. Getting to the edge of the Promised Land was no surprise; this is, after all, what the children of Israel had been working, and walking, toward for forty years. Yet there's no doubt that pulses quickened as the Israelites stood next to the Jordan River, contemplating the next steps that the Lord had in store for them.

Likewise, Jesus focused throughout His ministry on heading toward the cross. He alone was not surprised by the events that led in quick succession to acclamation in Jerusalem, agony and betrayal in Gethsemane, and then the horrific events culminating in Golgotha. Yet He too had to entrust the change that He faced—an agonizing, atoning death—to God the Father, to whom he prayed, "Into your hands I commit my spirit" (Luke 23:46). In both of these instances, the change is predictable and anticipated. That fact makes it no less momentous, but it does hold implications for guidance.

Scripture is replete with instances of the second kind of change, those developments that enter the lives of God's people totally without warning. One example comes at the beginning of Matthew's gospel: "[A]n angel of the Lord appeared to Joseph in a dream. 'Get up,' he said, 'take the child and his mother and escape to Egypt. Stay there until I tell you, for Herod is going to search for the child to kill him'" (Matthew 2:13). Like Gideon (see **Fleeces [33]**), Joseph is quietly getting on with life when God abruptly breaks in with unmistakable authority, telling him to take a bold step that will help accomplish God's purposes.

We can draw several lessons concerning guidance from these first two kinds of changes. One is that for the predictable changes, we can be preparing for them in prayer. Do we think that Joshua only began thinking and praying about entering the Promised Land when he reached its borders? Or that Jesus first prayed about being prepared for the cross only that night in Gethsemane? Likewise, we can prepare and pray for guidance long in advance of events we can expect to come our way. High school students, even though they may be thin on specifics, can pray generally about their choice of college or the best step to take after graduation. College students can pray about the steps to take after getting their degrees. Other changes may be heading our way, some unwelcome but inevitable, others that we eagerly anticipate. We will be better able to handle all of them by committing them to God, even far in advance, and asking for His wisdom so we may choose well when the time comes.

What of those dramatic moments of unexpected change? Again, the change could be welcome (an unexpected promotion) or unwelcome (the sudden death of a loved one). Either way, we may be called upon at a moment's notice to seek God's help in making major decisions. That's where various other sections in this book may be helpful, such as **Getting Ready for Guidance [24]; Guidance in a Crunch [37]; "Wit's End" Guidance [42]**.

A third category includes those slower, more incremental changes that arise out of everyday life. We slowly find ourselves becoming restless with our church, feeling we're getting less and less of the nurturing we need. Is it time to consider leaving? What are the implications for us, for our families, of such a change? Or should we stay, and if so, what are the implications of that? These kinds of changes aren't necessarily marked by a particular point in time, like a graduation date or the sudden shock of a phone call bearing bad news. They parallel the distinction that journalists make between hard news (or events) and trends. Particular events happen at a specific time: today's basketball game, tomorrow's city council meeting. Whether the news was anticipated or not, events are easy to cover. Trends, by contrast, are much more slippery and harder to detect and write about.

So it is with us. Because there may be no one point when we might say it's time to seek another church, we struggle to decide. Perhaps it's with these slow, incremental changes in our lives that we most need guidance—for God may be wanting us to change in areas we don't yet realize change is called for. Thus, our quest for guidance should be concerned for God to help us know where we should be sensitive to possible changes that we should be making.

Then there are the times when we ought *not* to change. Rather than leaving the church where we feel unhappy, maybe we should stick it out and make whatever contribution we can. By no means does God want us to see every unpleasantness or obstacle in life as a reason to change our circumstances. The difficulty is in knowing which unpleasant circumstances call for change and which call for endurance. That difficulty itself calls for another kind of discernment and guidance.

Change often brings discomfort or even pain. Charles Swindoll puts it this way: "God-sized assignments not only require trust, they also require major adjustments. I have never seen an exception to this rule: *Major adjustments accompany God's will.*" Even the most positive changes in our lives require adjustments and giving up something from our past.

Hence, a warning: Because change is so inextricably related to guidance, we need to not only prepare ourselves for the answers that God will give us, but also to be ready for the accompanying discomfort that will come from acting on these changes. This isn't pleasant news if you're someone who particularly dislikes change and is deeply comforted by the known and the familiar.

For our own spiritual growth, God requires that we keep growing and changing.

The Gospels and Epistles call us to a life of discipleship and ongoing spiritual growth; the New Testament repeatedly emphasizes that God doesn't call us to be static Christians. Whether that's dealing with normal spiritual growth or transitions brought on by life's circumstances, the sooner we recognize that change is a permanent feature of our Christian walk, the better we'll be able to grapple with those guidance issues that we encounter.

> ## The Serenity Prayer
>
> O God, grant us the serenity to accept what cannot be changed,
>
> the courage to change what can be changed
>
> and the wisdom to know the difference.
>
> —Reinhold Niebuhr

9 Clear Thinking

We don't serve a mindless God, and He expects us to mirror that part of His character by using our intellect to think through questions of guidance.

Charles R. Swindoll tells the story in *The Mystery of God's Will* of someone who was driving in Washington, D.C., when his car broke down outside the Philippine Embassy—something he took to be a sign that God wanted him to be a missionary to that country. In addition to criticizing this kind of thinking, which he describes as "voodoo theology," Swindoll helps illustrate the often mindless approach Christians bring to guidance.

> ## Godly Minds
>
> God guides through your heightened moral intelligence. "Can you not of yourselves judge that which is right?" said Jesus. He expected us to think our way through to right Christian conclusions.
>
> —E. Stanley Jones

You may not have realized this before, but an indispensable part of guidance is the sheer mental energy it typically demands. Quite apart from our commitment to working through **The Big Five [1]**, we need to bring to the guidance process a willingness to think—and to think clearly, with sustained effort. Curiously, Christians will sometimes pour their souls into seeking God's leading, prayerfully and earnestly seeking His will, but completely fail to do even the most elementary thinking about what is required of them. We therefore need to consider the following reasons why God expects us to bring significant thought to the guidance process, and consider briefly why Christians often fail to do so.

God made us to be thinking creatures and that's how we're supposed to function. Our capacity for astonishingly sophisticated thought is one of several qualities that makes humans unique among God's creatures. (Other qualities include our capacity for complex language and our ability to worship.) Therefore, it's unimaginable that God would expect Christians to ignore our ability to reason through the issues we face. On the contrary, He expects us to take it seriously. J. I. Packer puts it this way: "God made us thinking beings, and He guides our minds so that in His presence we think things out—no guidance otherwise!"

We need to be in tune with the more ordinary, routine, rational ways of discovering where God seeks to take us next.

Because guidance is normally a rational affair, we're likely to discover God's leading more easily if we accept how it works—and use the necessary tool, our minds, to do so. David Watson puts it well: "God wants us to use our minds and common sense, because guidance is usually thoroughly rational. In trusting the Holy Spirit we must be aware of super-spirituality which is always looking for the unusual in God's guidance."[1] As indicated elsewhere (**How God Guides [11]**), guidance is typically ordinary. Only rarely does God guide using **Signs and Wonders [39]**. For the most part, we need to be in tune with the more ordinary, routine, rational ways of discovering where God seeks to take us next, all of which require hard thought. Are there exceptions to this emphasis on rational guidance? Of course. F. B. Meyer says that "at times God may bid us act against our reason, but these are very exceptional; and then our duty will be so clear that there can be no mistake." He adds that for the most part God will speak through our careful thinking, and through our careful "weighing and balancing the pros and cons" of the issue we face. Finally, let's make no mistake: We're talking here about our minds working in conjunction with **The Big Five [1],** and being fully sensitive to what David Watson rightly emphasizes is the role of the Holy Spirit in steering our thinking. We're not suggesting

> ## The Music of Thought
>
> God has given us a brain and his Spirit to work in harmony and in concert.
>
> —Charles R. Swindoll

simply sitting down and thinking through what should be the next step. Anyone can do that. Christian guidance, by contrast, begins with and is grounded in The Big Five, and it is on this foundation that our thinking must proceed.

Not to turn to sound thinking and judgment insults God. If using clear thinking and sound judgment is a typical element in receiving God's guidance, we need to have good reason for ignoring His standard operating procedures. Because it's impossible to predict how God may choose to guide us in any and every circumstance, it's conceivable that at times He'll choose not to use His normal way of doing things. Should we think we're at one of those points, we ought to be sure that the overriding of "normal procedures" seems to be initiated by God, not ourselves. An example: Normally God would not tell us to marry a prostitute, yet for His own good reason He did exactly that to Hosea, making quite plain what the prophet ought to do. Almost all the time, however, God will expect us to use our common sense and sound judgment as we seek to honor Him through our lives. As we learn in the parable of the talents (Matthew 25:14-30), not to use what God has given us invites our Master's anger. Whether we're talking about using our minds in general or specifically to clarify a guidance issue, we do well to heed the warning of John Stott: "[W]e need to repent of the cult of mindlessness, and of any residual anti-intellectualism or intellectual laziness of which we may be guilty. These things are negative, cramping, and destructive. They insult God, impoverish and weaken our testimony. A responsible use of our minds, on the other hand, glorifies God, enriches us, and strengthens our witness in the world."

Sanctification slowly transforms our thinking to become more like God's. Just as Jesus' mind and will were in perfect harmony with His Father's, we too have—with the help of the Holy Spirit—the capacity to become more Christlike in living out His will.

Hence our increasing ability, as we mature in our faith, to say with a strange mix of confidence and humility that our thoughts *are* of God—at least, some of the time. Jesus prayed that His disciples "may be one, Father, just as you are in me and I am in you. May they also be in us so that the world may believe that you have sent me. I have given them the glory that you gave me, that they may be one as we are one: I in them and you in me" (John 17:21-23). As we deepen in our faith, we increasingly show that "oneness." We must not make the mistake of thinking that simply because certain thoughts came into our minds that they are by definition sinful. Yes, we always deal with the problem of **Mixed Motives [54],** but we irresponsibly toss out the doctrine of sanctification if we say that God can never use our minds and our thoughts to convey His will to us. The way our minds are becoming "Christianized" is, after all, exactly what Paul is speaking about in Romans 12:2: "be transformed by the renewing of your mind. Then you will be able to test and approve what God's will is—his good, pleasing and perfect will."

Not using clear thinking and sound judgment can discredit or embarrass God, His church, and ourselves. By abandoning what F. B. Meyer terms "sanctified common sense," we engage in potentially limitless foolishness. The example of the car breaking down outside the Philippine Embassy demonstrates what can happen when we throw out common sense. Derek Tidball, who formerly taught at the London Bible College, tells of a woman who was convinced God had guided her to apply to the college because she had seen a pile of bricks marked with the letters LBC. Not unkindly, he wondered why she couldn't equally well have seen that as God's leading to apply for work with the brick manufacturer, the London Brick Company, or even the London Broadcasting Company.[2]

The point is that Christians will sometimes disregard even the most basic common sense thinking, and base potentially major decisions on the flimsiest or even nonexistent reasoning. When any nonChristian would take at least some care in thinking through decisions, why do Christians at times engage in such mindlessness when we have at our disposal the guidance of God Himself? That question merits a few more paragraphs.

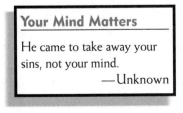

Your Mind Matters

He came to take away your sins, not your mind.
—Unknown

We may think that thinking isn't spiritual and has

little or no place in guidance. If that's our belief, we should reread John Stott's strong language previously quoted. As the preceding paragraphs indicate, that seriously misreads the way God sees the role of thinking.

Although we don't like admitting it, we may simply be lazy and wish to avoid anything resembling a mental workout. Such laziness may manifest itself in our thinking generally, or it may characterize the way we work through **The Big Five [1]**. M. Blaine Smith, for example, says, "We should avoid the crystal-ball approach to the Bible which looks for easy answers to difficult decisions and seeks to escape from our God-given responsibility for careful decision making."[3]

Whether we like it or not, we may have come to depend on a **Signs and Wonders [39]** *kind of guidance, with all the pitfalls that brings.* Perhaps we've come to expect that guidance isn't legitimate unless it has a Signs and Wonders dimension to it—that it needs to have something with a miraculous edge. So if we're contemplating mission work and our car breaks down outside the Philippine Embassy, or if we're thinking of training for the ministry and we see what surely must be a sign directly from God's hand, we need think no further. We needn't ask any more questions or think any further: The Signs and Wonders have spoken. Far from honoring God with our obedience to His leading, we're essentially relying on plain superstition, not a carefully considered, Spirit-led process of guidance. As Bruce Waltke writes in *Finding the Will of God: A Pagan Notion?,* "Don't fall into the trap of thinking that God's guidance will always be something spectacular or unique. Often he guides us by simply letting us use our heads."[4]

10 Doors—Open and Closed

Closed doors don't mean God never wants you to enter, open ones don't mean you should. (Or, before trying a door, see what you can learn by looking through a window.)

Christians spend plenty of time talking about doors. What we're really referring to is how we respond to the **Circumstances [5]** that have become part of God's guidance. While the circumstances that we face make up the bigger picture, what we call doors are the specific "yes" or "no" options that flow from these circumstances.

But what should you be concerned about with these yes or no options?

The first concern is, which doors should you be exploring in the first place? The answer is simple enough: Try the handles of any that seem to make sense to you after you've gone through as much of **The Big Five [1]** process as you can. It's important at this stage to remember the freedom you have, as described in the section titled **Do What You Like [31]**. If, for example, you're finishing high school or college, you've begun to identify possible next steps that match what you think God might be calling you to do, as well as noting which match your gifts, skills, and aptitudes. Your task now is to narrow those possibilities—initially to a few viable options and finally to one. As you consider different possibilities, you'll realize that some are more realistic than others. Some may hold particular appeal for you. The responsibility is yours, however, to walk around trying these door handles. It is *you* who need to see which doors are unlocked and which aren't; the doors aren't going to come to you. You need to be actively engaged in the guidance process in this highly practical way, just as you are actively engaged in seeking God's leading through Scripture and prayer.

The second question is harder to answer. If a door seems locked, how many times do you try it before you give up? At what point does great patience and persistence become pigheaded stubbornness? If you're convinced that God has called you to seminary to prepare for the pastorate, and it's a call that's reinforced by mature Christian friends and your church as a whole, what happens if each of the four seminaries you apply to this year rejects you? What if you apply again next year, maybe adding a few others to your list, and again each of them rejects you?

> ## Questions About "Closed and Open Doors"
>
> - Which doors should I be trying to open?
> - If a door seems closed, how long should I keep trying to get in?
> - Just because a door has opened, should I head inside?
> - What if I find myself in front of two or more open doors?

Do you try a third time? Do you keep trying until you're 67 years old, steadfast in your conviction that God has called you to head that way? You're not about to deny His call; you *know* He will honor your persistence.

There is no one answer to this kind of dilemma. Possible responses are to revisit the depth of your conviction that this is the right door to be trying. Maybe what you thought was God calling you to seminary was in fact Him calling you to full time youth work and not the pastorate. Perhaps He said "ministry" and you heard "pastorate." Or perhaps what you thought was God's call simply isn't; reviewing **Calling [44]** would at this point be helpful.

We can be sure, though, that if God is wanting us to fill a particular role in His kingdom, He will be opening the doors for us. Hannah Whitall Smith says, "If the Lord 'goes before' us, he will open the door for us, and we shall not need to batter down doors for ourselves."[5] If a door stays locked despite our repeated attempts to open it, we need to look seriously at two possibilities. The first is that we've misunderstood, and that God doesn't want us to head that way. Then it's time to give up and move on to other doors. The second is that He wants us to wait and try it later. Only you can know which of these two possibilities applies to you. G. Campbell Morgan says that "the Spirit never leads without opening the doors sooner or later."[6] If it's getting to be later and later, then it's important to ensure that we've not crossed the line between faithfully and patiently trying to honor God's will and stubbornly sticking to something as a matter of pride.

The third question has an easy answer: Just because a door has opened, should I assume that God wants me to head inside? Obviously not. Opportunities by themselves don't equate to God's will for your life. If you're a full-time college student and your wealthy Uncle Edgar suddenly invites you to join him on a six-week vacation in Europe, it would be irresponsible to drop out of school simply because you've been offered this opportunity. Similarly, if you're working happily at a particular job when, out of the blue, you're offered another (and better) one at a different company, that open door doesn't necessarily equate to God's will for your life. You have a score of questions still to ask, beginning with, "How does this opportunity fit into the big picture of God's will for my life?" and "How does this opportunity look against the backdrop of The Big Five?" Rushing through every door simply because it happens to be open is a manifestation of folly, not faith. For one thing, surely you'd want to have an informed view of where the door leads. Into what room will it take you? In brief, never assume that an open door necessarily has God's blessing on it. Taken out of the context of the guidance process, open doors don't necessarily have any importance — if anything, they could easily be distractions from what we are presently called to do. But when we find doors that are open, and everything else in that process is telling us it makes sense to walk on through, then it's time to take them seriously.

The fourth question considers what to do if you find yourself facing two or more open doors. Again, assuming you've reached that point as part of your overall quest for guidance, then you're in a fortunate position. You'll want to consider the nature of the options you face. (See **Choices, Choices [20].**) Remember as you process this decision that any one of these doors might be equally acceptable and pleasing to God.

Two final thoughts on opened and closed doors. Assuming you're convinced that an opened door is precisely where God wants you to go, beware of thinking that everything from now on will be clear sailing. It might not. "The open door," says G. Campbell Morgan, "does not necessarily mean the easy pathway. This is a common mistake. One has often heard persons say the way is made plain, and by 'plain' they mean easy. And yet . . . the most plain pathway has often been the most difficult."[7] (See **When Guidance "Goes Wrong" [59].**)

When a door closes, we need to rise above what may be our initial disappointment. As we look to God's bigger picture, we need to be grateful that He's steering us away from where we *thought* we might go to where we *should*. Writing in the context of finding the right job, Keith Miller says we should say a prayer of thanksgiving every time a door closes, because "every time you prove something is *not* feasible you are getting more into the world of real choices."

Getting to those real choices is precisely the point of trying the door handles. By making our door-opening exercise part of our overall search

> ## Why Do Doors Close?
>
> Not until we walk through the open door will we realize the necessity of the previously closed one.
> —Charles R. Swindoll

for God's will, we can know which are the doors to leave alone. We also will learn which are the doors where God bids us enter, as we step with confidence into the next stage of His will for our lives.

See also **Listening [13]; Testing, Testing [16]; Waiting [40]**.

11 How God Guides — Using "The Stuff of This World"

> **In the Face of Opposition**
>
> But I will stay on at Ephesus until Pentecost, because a great door for effective work has opened to me, and there are many who oppose me.
> — 1 Corinthians 16:8-9

While we can never predict the specifics of how God will guide in any given situation, we can be sure He will lead us far more often through means that are ordinary and predictable rather than spectacular.

Imagine that you've just finished a job interview. It went well, and the interviewer tells you, "I'll be in touch to let you know, one way or another." No time frame is mentioned, nor are you told how you might hear. As the days go by, you keep checking the mail, listening for the phone, or, if you gave your e-mail address, you keep checking that too. Or maybe this person will send you a fax. It's conceivable, but highly unlikely, that the interviewer will show up in person at your home to tell you you've got the job. Even more unlikely, someone dressed in a Viking outfit might burst into your living room tomorrow night to bring you the news. Possible, but unlikely.

So too with God. He's certainly a God of surprises, but He's also a God of great predictability. While we can never put limits on exactly how God may guide us at any time, the odds are high that He will use more rather than less conventional means. That means we're more likely to find His will for our lives through reading Scripture, prayer, the advice of others, or the circumstances of our lives. In other words, He's likely to use the four elements of **The Big Five [1]** that are external to us, elements that are part of the ordinary, everyday life of the Christian.

Elisabeth Elliot on How God Guides . . .

It is a scriptural principle that the divine energy acts upon the stuff of this world. Jesus had the servants fill the stone jars that happened to be standing there when he made wine from water at the marriage of Cana. He used a boy's lunch, instead of starting from nothing, to feed five thousand people. His own spittle and the dirt at his feet were the remedies for a blind man's eyes. Common things taken into the divine hands accomplished eternal purposes.

As a general rule, we can expect that principle to work with guidance too. God will typically use the ordinary "stuff" of our worlds to communicate His will to us. We can expect to hear His call through the "normal" channels of Christian living. Some or all of these avenues may contain Spirit-directed answers to our quest for guidance. Yet we are tempted at times to expect that God will send us **Signs and Wonders [39]** to leave us no doubt that it's His word we're hearing.

Perhaps it's our vanity that leads us to think (or secretly demand) that somehow we're special enough to deserve thunder-and-lightning level guidance. "Surely if God has something important to tell me," we think, "He's not going to use humdrum measures." So we expect that we're entitled to Moses-like personal encounters with God, or that we can expect to hear God's voice directly crying out from heaven, telling us which way to go.

Yes, at times God does use visions and dreams, or send angels to convey His word. Should He choose to communicate with us in such supernatural ways, He will. But just as we should never expect such dramatic and extraordinary means of guidance, so too should we be equally careful never to predict or limit how He might speak to us. Each of us is created as a unique being in God's image, and He honors that uniqueness in the ways He chooses to deal with us. In practice, though, God's guidance is likely to be far more ordinary than we might flatter ourselves into thinking we deserve. If the "stuff of this world" was good enough for Jesus to work

His divine purposes and miracles in the lives of those He met, we would do well to expect the same as He works out His purposes in our lives.

12 Intuition and Feelings

Intuition and feelings have a part to play in the guidance process, but the more you prize them the less value they have.

Although similar to **Inner Peace [6],** your intuition and feelings play a quite different role in guidance. Unlike Inner Peace, which serves as a confirming, affirming last step in **The Big Five [1],** the place of **Intuition and Feelings [12]** is far more murky, potentially confusing, or even downright misleading. Writers on guidance agree that, important though they may be to you, your emotions should play a minimal role in thinking through how God may be leading you.

Intuition, of course, is not the same as your feelings, and may (I repeat, *may*) have a helpful role. Your intuition at work may well be the prompting of the Holy Spirit, nudging you to act this way or that. When we're talking about concepts as intangible as one's intuition, "feeling led" or "having a hunch" about something, it's hard to know how much of these thoughts are God-initiated and shaped, and how much is simply our own thinking—or even wishful thinking. But if whatever you're thinking has any merit, it bears testing in other ways. How does it stack up against scriptural guidelines? Is this in accord with what other mature Christians might think? Could this thought or insight be an answer to prayer, and if so, how does it stand up to further prayer? What about the test of circumstances? In all these ways, intuition needs to be checked out as you address the question: Is this something that's a fleeting thought in the night, or is it a more significant and potentially important step in seeking God's will?

If you're someone for whom intuition plays an important role in life, listen all the more attentively. As you already have experience of how God uses intuition in guiding you, you have practice in knowing how best to listen. On the other hand, if this intuitive impulse is something new or out of the ordinary, it calls for all that much more care and scrutiny before you should feel free to act upon it. Intuition may well be used by God—but because it can easily be abused by us, it needs to be handled with great care.

What About Feelings?

When it comes to letting your feelings guide you, Eugene Peterson puts it quite bluntly: "Feelings are great liars." He adds: "Feelings are important in many areas, but completely unreliable in matters of faith." He quotes Paul Scherer as saying that "The Bible wastes very little time on the way we feel." And F. B. Meyer, in his classic *The Secret of Guidance*, writes: "Our feelings are very deceptive. . . . They are affected by the state of our health, changes in the weather, the society or absence of those we love." Feeling happy about a step you plan to take is no sure indication it is correct, and feeling unhappy (or simply neutral) is not necessarily telling you it's wrong.

A final thought on this topic. Perhaps you are by nature someone whose emotions are close to the surface and typically prominent in your thinking and decision-making. Are you simply to ignore this vital dimension of who you are as you seek God's leading? Of course not. Remember, though, that any quality of character or personality can become a weakness if it dominates other virtues. A decision that is "all heart" and "no head" may be no decision at all, but sheer impulsiveness. That's a far cry from the guidance you were presumably seeking when you opened this book.

13 Listening

Frank Laubach's advice on prayer is no more applicable than when we're seeking guidance: "Listening to God is far more important than giving him your ideas."

Waiting to hear God's voice in matters of guidance is clearly part of the **Prayer [3]** with which we should be surrounding our entire quest to know His will for us. The dimension of listening—actively, carefully, patiently—to what He wants to tell us is so important that it deserves special attention. The section on Prayer gives a more comprehensive overview of how we are to seek God's will. For now, it's important to emphasize four points that deal specifically with listening.

1. *Listening to God is far more important than giving Him your ideas.* A key part of prayer is approaching God with our requests. "Asking" flows easily and immediately out of us, especially if we are in times of great need. The part of prayer that we are far less naturally disposed to practice is the quiet listening for God's response. We live in a culture that is saturated with cell phones and e-mails, CNN broadcasts in airport lounges, and incessant demands for our attention from advertisers and others. We may struggle to hear God's voice through this clamor unless we deliberately give Him the quiet, undivided attention He needs to answer.

How might this happen? It might be through a regular time of devotions, Sunday worship, or a support or growth group we belong to. Or it might come through specially set aside time, like a personal retreat for a day or longer. That kind of time may not be available to us, but every one of us can surely commit to waiting on God five minutes a day when we face a guidance question—and proportionately more if we face a major one. As the section on prayer indicates, God has answers to our prayers. Are we patient enough to listen for them, rather than repeatedly telling God what He already knows?

2. *How will we know God's voice when we hear it?* Dallas Willard provides excellent answers to this question in his book, *Hearing God: Developing a Conversational Relationship with God.*

Paul Little on Listening . . .

Paul Little tells how as a university student he was deeply concerned to learn what God wanted him to do when he graduated. He was scurrying around campus, involved in one meeting after another, reading books and trying to find an answer. "I was doing everything but getting into the presence of God and asking him to show me." Then, he recalls, he attended the Urbana missions conference where a speaker asked, "How many of you who are concerned about the will of God spend five minutes a day asking him to show you his will?"

That question, Little said, dramatically refocused his thinking—on listening.[9]

> ## Listen Carefully
>
> Wait for your cues, and give them your full attention.
> — Yale Kneeland[9]

In brief, his point is that the better we come to know God, and the more our relationship with Him deepens and matures, the better we will be able to recognize His voice when He speaks to us. Just as we can immediately tell if the person on the phone is a loved one or someone else we know well, so too do we have the ability to recognize God's voice when He "calls." If you need assurance on this point, reread John 10, where Jesus speaks about "his sheep" recognizing the voice of the good Shepherd.

But for those of us who fear that our faith is still too uncertain to make that bold a claim, how can we be sure it's God's voice we're hearing, and not our own thoughts? How can we know it's God's will that's being presented to us, rather than our own wishful thinking? Willard is helpful on this point when he speaks of the various ways God speaks to us, including voices, dreams, and visions. His final category is pertinent here: "the human spirit or the 'still small voice.'" In trying to determine whether the "voice" we hear is in fact from God, Willard says that "for those who are living in harmony with God," His voice "most commonly comes in the form of their own thoughts and attendant feelings." He adds that this approach is best suited to God's redemptive purposes because "it most engages the faculties of free, intelligent beings involved in the work of God as his colaborers and friends." In other words, as we grow in our relationship with God and bring our minds and hearts increasingly under His influence in our lives, we will slowly become more Christlike in our own characters. As a result, our thoughts will become more like God's thoughts, and our will and desires will become more like God's will and desires. Because God made us as conscious, thinking beings, it is obviously through our minds and thoughts that He seeks to reach us. While the section on **Clear Thinking [9]** goes into more detail on the role our minds play in determining God's will, the point here is simply that we can and must expect to hear His voice through our own increasingly sanctified minds.

Few of us will feel bold enough to think we've arrived in this regard. At times it may seem we're definitely hearing God on a cell phone, but the line's so bad that we're missing part of the message. The static represents our limited ability always to hear clearly what God's saying. That may mean we need more listening, with additional "calls" to clarify His message. The point is that with patience and attentiveness, we *can* hear what God wants to tell us, and know with confidence it is His voice on the line. It is as if we have "Caller ID" and can tell easily who is on the line, even though the message isn't coming through as clearly as we'd like.

3. *The more we listen, the better we'll be at it.* If you've ever tried learning a new language, you know that the more you immerse yourself in the sounds of it being spoken all around you, for hours at a time, the better you become at hearing and understanding it. Likewise with the voice of God. The more we hear His voice, the easier it becomes to recognize it. If you have a favorite music group or a particular composer whose work you listen to repeatedly, eventually you're able to hear a certain distinctive quality to the music. God's voice too will slowly come to have its own distinctive quality.

4. *Simply listening for and recognizing God's voice is not enough; openness and obedience also are needed.* Numerous examples from Scripture make these points. The story of Samuel is especially helpful, because it tells of a young boy who "did not yet know the LORD: The word of the LORD had not yet been revealed to him" (1 Samuel 3:7). Samuel heard a voice that eventually spoke to him countless times in his life, but initially he didn't even know it was God talking to him. When he followed Eli's advice to reply to the voice by saying, "Speak LORD, for your servant is listening" (1 Samuel 3:9), he brought an openness to listening that was vitally important. Charles Martin points out that only when Samuel took this submissive stance "did God go on with the message."[10] Isaiah also models for us unconditional openness to whatever God wants to tell us. Only after he says "Here am I. Send me!" (Isaiah 6:8) does God tell him what to do. With Samuel, also, it was this openness to hearing that paved the way for building a profoundly close relationship with God.

Both Samuel and Isaiah also show us that the listening process must culminate in **Obedience [57]**. The child Samuel courageously acted on a

> ## Why We Pray
>
> The value of persistent prayer is not that he will hear us . . . but that we will finally hear him.
>
> —William McGill[11]

simple faith in response to God's voice and obeyed God by delivering His word to Eli. (See **Courage [47].**) Charles Martin says that "Faithful discharge of one message made Samuel ready for further growth." Both Samuel's and Isaiah's readiness to follow the listening with obedience throughout their lives made them two of Israel's leading prophets.

See also **How God Guides [11]; Waiting [40]; Mixed Motives [54].**

14 Maturity

As we grow in our faith, God expects us to mature in how we seek His guidance.

When I was a child, I talked like a child, I thought like a child, I reasoned like a child. When I became a man, I put childish ways behind me.
—1 Corinthians 13:11

Like the apostle Paul, we need to bring to our spiritual lives the qualities of adulthood, not those that marked the infant days of our faith. Unlike children, adults are expected to show qualities that include sound judgment, an appropriate level of independence, control over their emotions, and an acceptance of their responsibilities. Children simply are incapable of attaining these marks of maturity.

With our faith, too, we should give evidence of maturing as our Christian walks deepen. This maturity should also be reflected in the ways we seek God's guidance. As children, we're forever asking questions of our parents and teachers. As adults we keep asking questions, but the frequency, depth, and range of what we ask should be dramatically different. As children, we're forever asking for help. As adults, we remain dependent on others, but the kind of help we seek is presumably quite different.

So too with guidance. As our faith deepens, the quality and nature of our dependence on God should change significantly. Just as the way we practice **Obedience [57]** helps us obey next time around, so too does the way we experience guidance. The more we get to know God and how He directs our lives, the better able we are to hear Him next time, as the section on **Listening [13]** points out. When we're toddlers, our parents need to tie our shoelaces. But something's amiss if Mom and Dad still need to do that when we're fourteen. God too expects that as our faith grows, and as we get to know Him better, we will increasingly make decisions with confidence because our thinking and will are shaped by His mind and His will.

Clearly, the qualities of the mature Christian are what we should be aiming for, even though few of us attain such a level of spiritual sensitivity.

In addition to looking at this ideal picture that White presents (see box), we do well to consider how mature Christians ought *not* to behave. As Oswald Chambers writes in his classic *My Utmost for His Highest*, "We have to be so one with God that we do not continually need to ask for his guidance. Sanctification means that we are made the children of God, and the natural life of a child is obedience—until he wishes to be disobedient." Adults who have healthy, loving relationships with their parents aren't turning to them every five minutes to ask for help; but they don't hesitate either to bring to their parents any serious issues on which they seek advice or other help.

Donald Coggan, the former Archbishop of Canterbury, says that guidance takes different forms as we grow. When we're children, he says, it comes mostly in the form of directions: "Shut the door quietly. Wash your hands." But as we become adults, he notes, parents interact with their children on a much different level. "It is more the interplay of a mature mind on a less fully matured one. It is the sharing of wisdom with one less deeply experienced. It is still needed, but the form of guidance has changed from that of earlier years."

Our relationship with God ought to be far closer, of course, than even the warmest son- or daughter-relationship with a parent. But that relationship models well what we should expect from a mature faith. Again, the insight of Oswald

> ## Grasping God's Heart
>
> God does not desire to guide us magically. He wants us to know his mind. He wants us to grasp his very heart. We need minds so soaked with the content of Scripture, so imbued with biblical outlooks and principles, so sensitive to the Holy Spirit's prompting that we will know instinctively the right steps to take in any circumstances, small or great.
>
> —John White

Chambers: "At first we want the consciousness of being guided by God, then as we go on we live so much in the consciousness of God that we do not need to ask what his will is, because the thought of choosing any other will never occur to us."

The standard Chambers presents us is daunting. We see it modeled in Jesus, and that must therefore be our goal too. But living at such a level of spiritual depth and maturity, so that we know instinctively how God would have us act, is precisely that—a *goal*, not a *requirement*, in our faith journeys. God doesn't demand the fullest levels of maturity in our responses to His guidance, but He does expect that we're moving toward the highest levels of spiritual maturity we're capable of. And we should settle for nothing less.

15 Perfect Plans

While God's plans are perfect, His love, patience, and boundless imagination lead Him to redraw those plans for our lives whenever necessary.

Whatever plans God has for our lives *are* perfect—precisely because they're *His* plans. The idea of God's "perfect plan," however, can be a barrier in our thinking if we don't use His plans as He wants us to. We can't know in any detailed or complete way what His overall plan is. All we can know is God's general will, which He wants not only for our lives but for all of His children, as well as His specific will for *the next step* in our lives. (See **God's Will [25].**)

Our focus should thus be on those parts we can know: God's general expectation of us that we live holy lives and that we become more and more like Christ, and honor Him in the step-by-step specifics of living out our individual circumstances. Put differently, God isn't nearly as concerned with us following some kind of plan as He is with what kind of people we become. John Ortberg says that "God's purpose in guidance is not to get us to perform the right actions. His purpose is to help us become the right kind of people." Obviously, God cares that we do the right things and about whom we become. But if we're inclined to focus on what God wants us to *do* and neglect what He wants us to *be*, then Ortberg's words are a helpful corrective.

We don't need to know anything more about God's plans than the next step He wants us to take. In fact, we needlessly frustrate ourselves if we want God to show us His big picture plans for us. That's simply not how He reveals His plans to His children. We need to beware of thinking that we need God's full, detailed plan before we can live our lives in obedience to Him. The Introduction presented the picture of God as the architect helping us build our lives in a way that will please Him. While it would be great to get a set of architect's drawings that show the end result, God doesn't communicate to us exactly what final shape our lives will take. Instead, God says, "Put this brick here. Now this one, over there." And so we build, knowing we're following the principles of good construction that are mirrored in God's general will, and with the attention to detail that flows from His particular will for our lives.

One of the hang-ups we bring to this building process is our fear of making mistakes. What if we put 100 bricks over here instead of where He told us? We can't undo what we've done. But we can have the fullest confidence in an Architect who can work even our biggest blunders into a house whose completed design will be flawless. God is perfectly able to work our limitations and our times of disobedience into His purposes. If we're seriously committed to following Him and honoring Him in the choices we make, then by the end of our days God will have helped us build a life that looks as if it was planned exactly that way from the beginning.

> **The Walk of Faith**
>
> God doesn't seem to favor giving blueprints. On the contrary, he seems to tell us to go a step at a time and trust him for the rest. I suppose that is what is meant by the walk of faith — not a key to unlock the future, but a torch to light up the path, a path wide enough for two, for him and you to walk together.
>
> —Donald Coggan

16 Testing, Testing

If what seems like guidance is indeed from God, it can stand testing.

If you sense that you are to take action X or make decision Y, that conviction should be able to withstand the careful scrutiny of The Big Five. Sometimes a deadline looms and such testing simply isn't possible. But when time permits, it's well worth checking out what you think the Lord is telling you or where He is leading.

One reason is simply to ensure, as best you can, that you *are* right. It may happen that as you take one or more of the following steps suggested below that you suddenly realize you had misread your cues after all. Now is the time to do such confirming and affirming of your course. If you realize some aspect of the guidance you were going to pursue is flawed, it's better to recognize that now (and if necessary admit it to others), and go back a square or two—or even back to square one if necessary.

In addition, testing what you believe to be God's leading is helpful if doubts or difficulties arise later. If you've concluded that God is leading you where to go, and then you double-check that conviction, you'll have added confidence that you're on the right road when hard times come. As **Doubts [48]** and **When Guidance "Goes Wrong" [59]** make clear, difficulties will arise at times; when they do, knowing we acted on guidance that was solidly grounded will provide valuable assurance.

J. Oswald Sanders points to yet another reason for testing the guidance we've received: our motives. Because we are so capable of deceiving ourselves and engaging in wishful thinking when it comes to hearing God's leading, he offers an important warning: "If disappointment, trouble, frustration, or failure have influenced our decision, we should be doubly careful before acting on it." (See **Mixed Motives [54]**.)

Testing is not without its dangers. We can abuse the process of testing what God has shown us if our real motives are actually a dithering indecisiveness, plain fearfulness, or perhaps a reluctance to obey. Another abuse of testing is when we seek one confirmation after another of what God has plainly revealed. When Jesus rebuffs Satan by telling him in Matthew 4:7, "Do not put the Lord your God to the test," He's quoting Deuteronomy 6:16. Interestingly, the next few verses in Deuteronomy make it clear how God expects Israel simply to obey what they already know to do: "Be sure to keep the commands of the LORD your God and the stipulations and decrees he has given you. Do what is right and good in the LORD's sight, so that it may go well with you" (Deuteronomy 6:17-18).

Testing Your Guidance

How do you test the guidance you have before you? Three reliable ways are to revisit the basics, to pray, and to wait.

1. The first step is to assess once again the move you are about to take through the grid of **The Big Five [1].** Yes, you've no doubt already done this once, twice, or even more. But one last check won't hurt.
2. The second option of course is to continue to pray about the step ahead. As you seek to confirm God's leading on the issue you're facing, you're inviting Him to set you straight if you're in danger of making a wrong move.
3. Finally, if you have time on your side, you may be able to wait to see if what seems like the correct course right now still looks that way next week or next month. If it's a decision that doesn't have to be made now, why *not* wait?

Having done all that, you're able to move forward with heightened confidence that you're heading in the right direction—or else, to your surprise and relief, you've found an even better way.

See also **Guidance in a Crunch [37]; Waiting [40].**

17 Wisdom

Godly wisdom—knowing what God would have us do next—is a synonym for guidance.

When we seek God's guidance, we're really concerned about taking the next step. That also happens to be a pretty good definition of wisdom. Scripture is replete with references to wisdom, both as a quality that is central to God's character and as an attribute Christians should seek. But it's not "wisdom" as referred to in ordinary conversation to which we should aspire. Rather, the emphasis is on godly wisdom. To oversimplify the difference, "ordinary" wisdom is being smart enough to know what to do next; godly wisdom is being smart enough to know what God wants us to do next. Thus, godly wisdom is infused with the leading of the Holy Spirit.

Cherish Wisdom

Get wisdom, get understanding;
do not forget my words or swerve from them.
Do not forsake wisdom, and she will protect you;
love her, and she will watch over you.
Wisdom is supreme; therefore get wisdom.
Though it cost you all you have, get understanding.
—Proverbs 4:5-7

It's interesting how often God tells us to seek after wisdom, something that emerges in any careful reading of Scripture. Because few of us regard ourselves as having the godly wisdom we need to make tough choices, what are we to do? How do we acquire the wisdom we're urged to embrace? The short answer is that we grow in wisdom the same way we grow in faith—by living it out. By following the principles outlined in **The Big Five [1]**, and grounding all we do in our commitment to God, we're showing that "The fear of the Lord is the beginning of wisdom, and they who live by it grow in understanding" (Psalm 111:10, REV). Like living a life of faith, we get better at living out godly wisdom simply with practice. By seeking after it and then nurturing it day by day, year by year, slowly we will grow in wisdom.

> ## Acting Wisely
>
> It is characteristic of wisdom not to do desperate things.
> —Henry David Thoreau

Facing a tough decision right now? Afraid that you're sorely lacking in the wisdom department? None of us ran before we walked, and it's the same with wisdom. To state the obvious, we can't start where we are not. We need to begin with what we have. As in the parable of the servants with the talents (Matthew 25), by using what we have, we'll grow our capacity to make wiser decisions in the days ahead. Meanwhile, we're to act with a confident humility, seeking always to bring a godly wisdom to the task at hand. Then we can be assured that if we're doing other things right, God will give us the degree of wisdom befitting our need.

Solomon's Prayer for Wisdom

Now, O LORD my God, you have made your servant king in place of my father David. But I am only a little child and do not know how to carry out my duties. Your servant is here among the people you have chosen, a great people, too numerous to count or number. So give your servant a discerning heart to govern your people and to distinguish between right and wrong. For who is able to govern this great people of yours?
—1 Kings 3:7-9

See also **Maturity [14].**

Today is mine. Tomorrow is none of my business. If I peer anxiously into the fog of the future, I will strain my spiritual eyes so that I will not see clearly what is required of me now.

Elisabeth Elliot

Trust in Him

Understanding God's Will

18 The "Abba, Father" Principle

God's guidance is that of a loving, involved parent who seeks nothing but our best.

One of the most important concepts to grasp about guidance is that of God as "Daddy." Even more than the wisest and most loving of earthly parents, God seeks our very best—hiding nothing from us and holding nothing back. If we can accept this principle of His boundless love for us, much else about guidance falls into place. For example, if God seeks our best, we can dump forever the silly notion that He somehow plays games with us when we seek to know His will. It's not as if He's hidden His "perfect will" behind the recliner, and as we stumble around the living room He tells us "warm, warmer, no, now you're getting colder." Just because His will may not be easy to discern doesn't mean He's toying with us.

Even when we're bewildered over what God is doing in our lives, and we verge on despair as we can't understand where to turn, we can cling unswervingly to this reality: His parent-like love for us is infinitely greater than we can imagine, and we can trust Him to the fullest. He doesn't just point the direction (in His own way and in His own time), He also accompanies us on the journey.

Elisabeth Elliot on God's Guidance . . .

Writer Elisabeth Elliot, whose husband Jim was a missionary martyred in Ecuador in 1956, has referred to trips she has subsequently made through that country's dense forests: "I would far rather have a guide than the best advice or the clearest set of directions." God, she said, is that kind of guide, who doesn't just tell us the way. Like a parent helping a four-year-old learn to ride a bike, He's right beside us, encouraging us and ensuring that we don't fall.

Donald Coggan on Jesus Calling God "Father" . . .

To him that presumably conjured up a figure who loved and cared for his children. Their good was his great concern—their eternal welfare. That might—in fact would—include discipline. But surely, also, it would include guidance. A father who did not seek to guide his children would scarcely deserve the name of father.

Maybe you experienced a "trust walk" at a camp or youth group where you were blindfolded and then led on a potentially hazardous pathway by someone who held your hand or called out directions. The lesson being taught about God's willingness and ability to guide us, despite our limited capacity to see potential dangers, always came through clearly. Yes, it is we who need to do the walking, the living out of our lives, but it is He who guides. If a fellow camper is concerned enough to steer us away from the hazards and toward safety, how much more would God Himself direct our paths?

Many of us may not have known a loving, caring biological father. Or perhaps we still carry the emotional scars inflicted by an abusive mother. For such Christians, the picture of God as a loving, tender parent may be a barrier rather than a comfort. But whatever the limitations and failings of our earthly parents, we can know that God's love and leading never let us down. It wasn't by chance that Jesus taught us to pray, "Our Father . . ." He used language and imagery that, in the Aramaic language He spoke, captured the closeness and tenderness of a father as a loving "daddy." This quality of God the Father was foremost in His mind—and this image should be foremost in our minds too when we think of our need for guidance.

> ### An Earthly Comparison
>
> "If you, then, though you are evil, know how to give good gifts to your children, how much more will your Father in heaven give good gifts to those who ask him!"
>
> —Matthew 7:11

19 The Ambassador Principle

Paul said, "We are therefore Christ's ambassadors" (2 Corinthians 5:20). Christians who take seriously this view that we are ambassadors for Christ must be ready to act upon new orders to move to another posting at short notice.

Oswald Chambers, in *My Utmost for His Highest*, described what God expects of us: "I reckon on you for extreme service, with no complaining on your part, and no explanation on mine." As ambassadors for Christ, those are precisely our conditions of service. The role of the ambassador, though, is a curious one, because we are at the same time endowed with great authority yet are completely powerless. As God's people, placed carefully where He wants us, we have the fullest access to all the power we need to accomplish His purposes. Similarly, ambassadors for the United States or any other country act knowing they have the full authority of a government back home to support their actions. In the same way, Christians can live out God's will for their lives knowing it is in keeping with the overarching, eternal purposes that He has promised He will bring about.

Yet at the same time, both ambassadors of the government and of Christ are powerless in important respects. They can't set their own agendas, saying or doing whatever they please; they're required to follow instructions and directions from the head office. Nor can they simply choose to move from one setting to another. (The U.S. government would not take kindly to a fax from its ambassador to Belgium announcing that he or she had decided to move to Bolivia or Botswana, where the weather was warmer.) Nor does the Christian who takes seriously his or her role as ambassador move without orders from headquarters. Both kinds of ambassadors also lack any expectation of permanence or comfort. Career diplomats in the U.S. State Department go where they're assigned—sometimes to exotic, intriguing, and safe locations, other times to places that are bleak or dangerous. But whatever the task, good ambassadors don't question their posting because they know it is where their governments need them. They accept too that at any time they're subject to being reassigned, again depending on their governments' needs.

Likewise with an ambassador for Christ. Taking guidance seriously means living out our Christian discipleship empowered by God, and being completely and unquestioningly accepting of the conditions of service. These include knowing that any day you could awaken to a fax from God, telling you to prepare to move to Boston or Buffalo, Bolivia or Botswana—wherever you're needed next. The career diplomat begins packing and focusing on the next assignment and opportunity to serve. So should the "career Christian" for whom an answered prayer may have brought an unexpected turn. See also **Obedience [57].**

> ## Demands? Rights?
>
> The demand to know where we are going is one which no Christian has a right to make.
>
> —Lesslie Newbigin

20 Choices, Choices

Not all choices are created equal; sometimes we must choose between good and bad options, sometimes between good and equally good, and sometimes the choices are so minor that they really don't matter.

As you approach a decision, it's important to know what type of choice you're facing. Choices can be categorized in several ways. One schema by M. Blaine Smith refers to a broad distinction between moral choices and nonmoral ones. Moral choices are those that we address by one or more moral principles, such as love, justice, fairness, and so on. At the other end of the spectrum are choices that have no moral content or implications for us—for example, whether to have peanut butter or jelly (or both) on a sandwich. Smith describes how choices range from one type to the other, using five categories. The list below closely follows his:

1. Straightforward Moral Decisions
2. Complicated Moral Decisions
3. Gray Area Decisions
4. Complex Decisions
5. Straightforward Nonmoral Decisions

Many decisions we make are so easy that they demand little or no thought; in fact, they're not really decisions at all. These choices are in fact non-choices for the Christian. For example, Scripture has a strong prohibition on adultery. If we're tempted to break our marriage vows, we face a straightforward, clear-cut decision. Dealing with this or other temptations may not be easy, but at least the choice we face is plain. We obey God, or we don't; we choose a moral course, or we don't. Morally there isn't a choice at all. We're in a situation where one moral principle (faithfulness) overrides all rationalizations we try to bring to this temptation.

With more complicated moral decisions, however, we face a conflict between at least two moral principles. The classic example is the tension a judge faces in a mercy killing case, in which someone has murdered a relative to end a life filled with unrelenting and excruciating pain. The judge is torn between justice and mercy, needing to enforce a law that upholds the value of human life. At the same time, the judge also recognizes that the "killer" is not a violent threat to society.

Or what about the choice facing a couple who is increasingly troubled by the direction their church's youth program is taking? Do they stay and do what they can to help (loyalty), or leave because of concern for their own children (love)? This is the arena of hard ethical choices. The section on **Godly Decision Making [36]** offers ideas for how to resolve them.

The gray areas noted in category three are ones in which Christians have some degree of choice. Smith mentions the example from Romans 14:2, about whether Christians should eat meat that may have been offered to idols. Today, such gray areas include the behavior of drinking alcohol. Committed Christians would argue on either side of this issue. Some say that drinking responsibly is perfectly acceptable; others argue that drinking any alcohol sets a bad example for one's children, other Christians, and especially for nonChristians. "Gray area" decisions, in other words, are those where thoughtful Christians will disagree.

Complex decisions are typically those where we find ourselves needing to choose between options that are equally acceptable to God.

Of special interest to us is Smith's fourth category, complex decisions. "These are important personal decisions which have to do with more than merely matters of moral behavior," he says. "Complex decisions include major questions such as what profession to choose, what college to attend, whether and whom to marry and where to go to church. They also include decisions about priorities: How should you spend your time and money?" While these decisions certainly have a moral dimension to them, "moral principles will not finally settle these questions." In this area, scriptural principles are more helpful in giving us guidance.

As the section on **Do What You Like [31]** makes clear, certain activities are simply off limits to Christians. Scripture is helpful in those choices that deal with the general will of God. But we can't expect general scriptural principles to be as helpful when it comes to seeking God's specific will for our lives, as discussed in **God's Will [25]**. Therefore, complex decisions are typically those where we find ourselves needing to choose between options that are equally acceptable to God. He needs both accountants and archivists. But when we get to the particular needs of our situation, which is the better choice? When each seems compatible with God's will, how can we know which way to go? We'll return to this question later.

Finally, Smith refers to straightforward nonmoral decisions. He says, for example, that "no biblical principle applies to whether I wear a blue shirt today or a yellow one. This is a very simple decision and one which is clearly nonmoral in nature." Phillip Jensen and Tony Payne describe nonmoral decisions as belonging in what they call a "Who Cares?" category.[1] They're discussed in **Trivial Pursuit [27].** Occasionally, things that obviously seem to fit in the nonmoral category may, with a change of context, suddenly take on moral dimensions. For example, serving me hamburgers if I am a guest at your home may seem normal enough. But if you know I'm a vegetarian—and still you choose to serve me meat—that would be a deliberate insult, and obviously an act with moral implications.

Seeking God's will for our lives typically involves the complex decisions, a category that parallels what Jensen and Payne call "Wise and Unwise" decisions. Some choices can clearly be settled by biblical principles and lend themselves more to right/wrong or yes/no answers. Those choices that fall within God's will, however, call for our wisdom and diligence as we work through **The Big Five [1]** in seeking God's specific will for our lives. While it's within God's general will for someone to be either an accountant or an archivist (nothing in Scripture would steer us away from either choice), which is the better choice for *me?*

Jensen and Payne say that "if a decision is a matter of *wisdom,* then we should seek the counsel of the Scriptures and make our choice, without feeling guilty that we might be making the 'wrong' choice. If it's not in the right/wrong category, then we can't make the 'wrong' choice. Choosing either course is perfectly right and pleasing to God." The key here is to make that choice having sought God's wisdom in prayer and through Scripture. Having taken that step, we face far more freedom than we might have realized.

God—Abundant and Great

God is the God of abundance. There are twelve baskets full of pieces of bread left over. In life's decisions, God doesn't always bring us into places where all choices are between right and wrong. In his greatness, his children often find themselves in the enviable position of choosing among two or more rights! It would have been right to take any one of the pieces of bread that Christ multiplied.

—Jay Adams

More important still is for us to know what type of choice we're dealing with in the first place. The philosopher John Dewey said, "Outline a problem as clearly as possible and you've already half-solved it." The result may be even better with guidance: Clarify the kind of choice you're facing, and you may just have made your decision.

21 Conditional Guidance

God's guidance isn't like a legal contract, but it still comes with conditions; read the bold print about what He expects of us.

This book assumes that you're serious about seeking God's will for your life, and that you're committed both to learning what God wants you to do and to acting on what you learn. When you approach that first step, it's helpful to remember that God's guidance comes with strings attached. Some of these conditions may seem obvious, but they're worth revisiting if, for whatever reason, you're encountering roadblocks or other hurdles as you seek God's leading.

Typically, you should meet each of the following five conditions before you can expect that God will speak, and that you'll hear Him. But that's not always the case. For example, the apostle Paul was hardly predisposed to seeking what we understand as Christian guidance when God intruded in his life in the most dramatic fashion. God speaks at times to some Christians with similar directness, even when they're not seeking any particular guidance. By and large, however, we can assume that the conditions listed below need to be honored if we're to be as open as possible in perceiving what God would have us do.

1. We must believe that God Himself will guide us. This requires understanding God and His character. Elisabeth Elliot says, "If we want to know what to do, we need to know first who will tell us." That means believing that the One who will tell us knows best and desires the best for us, and is eager to guide us. (See **The "Abba, Father" Principle [18].**) More important than knowing what God is concerned to do for us is the need to get to know *Him;* by doing so we'll far better understand the source and purposes underlying the guidance we'll receive. Phillip Jensen and Tony Payne write in *The Last Word on Guidance* that "If we understand God—what he's like, what motivates him, and what his plans are—we will be well on the way to understanding his guidance."[2]

2. *We must believe that we are capable of receiving God's guidance.* While we may accept this in theory, we may struggle genuinely to believe that we are capable of hearing what God wants to tell us. For a range of reasons, described in **Five Groundless Fears [49]**, we may have our doubts. We may simply believe we're just not good enough to deserve or recognize His guidance. In one respect, that's perfectly true. Our sinful natures, our mixed motives, our propensity to advance our will rather than God's— all these and other factors make it seem unlikely that He would want to guide us in the first place, or that we'd hear Him if He did. Yet that is exactly the wonder of guidance. Beyond God's readiness to guide, as described above, another obvious pre-condition to hearing God's voice is simply to believe that we're *able* to hear what He's saying. Even if our faith is lacking, God will take what little faith we have to help our hearing. Like the father of the boy with an evil spirit described in Mark 9, we too must say to Jesus, "I do believe; help me overcome my unbelief!" Still, other barriers may remain. There may be a lack in our seriousness about seeking God's will that makes us incapable of hearing Him. Or it may be that we're bringing such tainted motives to the process that we block out what God would tell us.

3. *We must in fact want God's leading.* If we have doubts about our openness to God's leading, we ought to bring these honestly before Him. Seeking God's leading always entails risks; we can have no idea where He may take us.

> ## Honest Self-Assessment
>
> I must honestly assess where I am in my relationship with God, what my emotions and circumstances reveal about my decision-making process, and where my desire to control is gridlocking my ability to follow his leading.
>
> —Dudley Delffs

Changes in our lives can be fearful—both those that we think we can predict and those that will take us into unknown territory. (See **Change [8].**) We can have understandable reasons for resisting any movement from where we are in our lives right now; the familiar, even with all its problems, is often preferable to the unknown. It's understandable that we may resist the idea of God moving us from where we are. For those of us at that point, F. B. Meyer says, "If you are not willing, confess that you are willing to be made willing."

4. We must show that we are serious about God's will by doing now what He's already given us to do. Alan Redpath said, "Don't expect God to reveal his will for you next week until you practice it today." If we aren't obeying God in our current Christian walk, how can He expect us to be serious about any other guidance He may give us? If we're not doing what we already know to be God's will, our priority must be repentance and getting our spiritual house in order before we think of any further guidance. The concern here, in other words, is about *present* obedience as a condition for guidance.

5. We must be completely open, in advance, to acting upon whatever God may tell us, unwelcome or unpleasant though it may be. In other words, we must be completely willing to set aside our wills, and to respond obediently to doing whatever God shows us to do. After hearing God's word, we're called upon to act. Lewis Sperry Chafer has written, "His leading is only for those who are already committed to do as he may lead." If we are potentially reluctant to following through on what He reveals to us, it's quite possibly part of a pattern in our lives that reveals less than a full commitment to honoring His will. The concern here is with *future* obedience. If we have a mixed record of following through on guidance, God may seek to work on our basic obedience before He can take us further in our Christian walk.

> ## A Prayer for Guidance
>
> My Father, I abandon myself to you. Do with me as you will.
> Whatever you may do with me, I thank you.
> I am prepared for anything, I accept everything.
> Provided your will is fulfilled in me and in all creatures I ask for nothing more, my God.
>
>   —Charles de Foucauld

22 The Consistency Principle

While we can never predict exactly how God may guide, we know His guidance will never contradict His Word or His character.

Have you heard the question about whether God could make a rock so large that He couldn't lift it? For some of us, that may have been the first time we thought about the consistency of God's nature, and whether His infinite power allowed Him to contradict Himself. We know the answer: God cannot and will not contradict His own nature. Quite apart from any other implications that this reality has for our relationship with Him, it offers us great comfort in the realm of guidance. We know that we can depend on His dependability. We know that what God's Word says, what He has told us in answering prayer, and what He has shown us through the circumstances over which He has sovereign control will all form part of a whole. We can be confident that, as Hannah Whitall Smith has written, these various voices—together with our sense of inner peace—"will necessarily harmonize, for God cannot say in one voice that which he contradicts in another."[3]

If we're getting conflicting readings in the guidance process, we need to remember that there's a difference between the readings our instruments give us and what they're actually measuring. Just as we may misread a compass, or the device could behave erratically, we still know that what it's trying to read is still reliable: true north is still out there, even if we can't detect it right now. Or perhaps we're sailboat purists, navigating by the stars when cloud cover prevents us from seeing clearly what course to chart. Even though we can't see the North Star right now, it's still there, as reliable as ever.

Likewise with guidance. Just as we may have misread the compass, or the clouds are preventing us from getting a good look at the North Star, so too we may be unable to bring together all the elements we need—at least, not yet. We know with complete confidence that the unchanging standards by which we want to steer remain as dependable as ever. We know too that just as the compass and the stars are not going to send us contradictory messages, with one pointing us north and the other east, so too God's guidance will point us in one direction in a way that's consistent with who He is.

23 The Future

Guidance is by definition concerned with the future, but with only one piece at a time.

The very nature of seeking God's will is that we're looking at what He wants us to do *next*. And "next" is exactly what God has in mind too. It's important, though, to look at three categories of "next," only one of which has to do with guidance.

The first is the step that lies immediately ahead in our lives. Then come the subsequent steps that He has in store for us. Lastly, there is God's ultimate purpose, not just for us, but for His kingdom as a whole—the final ushering in of His kingdom at the end of time.

Of these three, only the first concerns us here. God reveals His purposes for our lives one step at a time. Rarely does He give us any long-term view of what He has in mind for us.

Sometimes God presents people with the big picture of the work He has for them, as He did with Moses. Like him, you too may well be right in believing God is calling you to a task that is still a long time off. For example, it could be to work as a medical missionary. Strictly speaking, though, what He's really guiding you to do is excellent work in your high school science classes, or going on that health-related mission project during your college vacation, or applying to one particular medical school rather than another. Each of these actions is, of course, leading you toward your goal, one that you might well attain. On the other hand, it may be that while you're in med school you discover you're greatly gifted as a researcher, and unexpectedly find that God opens doors to lead you in directions you never anticipated.

> ## One Step at a Time
>
> God . . . only undertakes that *the steps* of a good man should be ordered by the Lord. Not next year, but tomorrow. . . . If you expect more than this, you will be disappointed.
> —F. B. Meyer

Not that we should forget our goals and abandon what we think God has called us to. Far from it. The point is simply that we need to move forward in humility and in openness, never insisting on what God will do with our lives in five or ten years time. As we trust Him fully to lead us step by step by step to live out the purposes He has for us, we should remember that a change of orders could arrive at any time. As we obey those orders, one faith-filled move at a time, we will one day arrive in God's presence. Then, as we step into eternity, we will see our futures as He had planned them all along.

See **The Ambassador Principle [19]; Obedience [57].**

24 Getting Ready for Guidance

Be at work now cultivating those qualities that will enable God to guide you more easily in the future.

Firefighters, SWAT teams, and emergency room doctors share a need for extensive training. They put in endless hours of preparation for the kinds of high stakes, often life-and-death situations that are inherent in their work. The decision making and choices that Christians encounter seldom rise to the dramatic level that face emergency professionals. What does apply, however, is the need for training.

The rest of this book emphasizes the need to decide wisely, in a way that pleases God, and to know how to do that. Just as important is *preparing* to make decisions. Whether we're looking at the expected or unexpected decisions we will face, how we have prepared for those moments of choosing is crucially important. If we've been living godly lives, attentive to God's leading day by day, in the ordinary and routine walk of Christian discipleship, we will be well attuned to receiving God's guidance at those special moments when we need it.

Ken Edgecombe writes that before we make a particular choice, our hearts have already been aligned in one direction or another. "Few of our choices are really spur-of-the-moment ones," he says. "What we end up doing is usually not too far removed from what we want to end up doing."

If we've living our Christian lives halfheartedly, when a major decision comes our way we're not going to be as "spiritually fit" as we should be in responding. If we're spiritually flabby and haven't been practicing our listening for God's voice, we'll find it harder to hear Him when we really need to.

Getting ready for guidance is no great mystery. It's a matter of living a Christian walk that steadily draws us closer to God and makes us

> ### Tuning in to God
>
> It is the law of life that we hear what we have trained ourselves to hear; day by day we must listen to God, so that day by day God's voice may become . . . clearer and clearer until it becomes the one sound to which above all our ears are attuned.
>
> —William Barclay

increasingly like Christ. That's the kind of Christian walk that Dallas Willard describes in his book *Hearing God—Developing a Conversational Relationship with God*. His point is that it is only by continuously deepening our relationship with God that we will hear His voice more clearly.

Understanding Christian discipleship, with its demands of obedience and faithfulness, is of course far simpler than living it out. As we grow in our faith and our Christian walk matures, we are likely to find ourselves used by God in new and deeper ways. As we make ourselves increasingly available to God, and as we trust Him more and more, we become equipped for more tasks that He has for us.

What is it we are getting ready for? We can't know. For the most part, it's the ordinary day-by-day decisions and choices we are called upon to make. Writing in his book, *The Will of God as a Way of Life*, Jerry Sittser says: "Who we choose to become and how we choose to live every day creates a trajectory for everything else."[4] In other words, our small daily choices determine the kinds of people we are—and, over time, our capacity to hear God's leading and live it out. Christian character isn't built overnight. But an ever-maturing Christian character needs to be in place if we're to respond optimally to guidance issues when they arise.

Sometimes, as the section on **Change [8]** notes, we face long-anticipated turning points or crossroads in our lives. Then there are also the totally unexpected challenges or even crises when we urgently seek and need God's leading. For most of us, these crises will seldom be three-alarm fires, a hostage situation, or a gunshot victim in the emergency room. But like people whose work routinely requires them to deal with such situations, Christians too should always be in a state of readiness—and for us that means being spiritually alert and fit. We don't know what opportunities or challenges God may bring our way tomorrow or the day after. We do know, however, that our overall "spiritual wellness" and the quality of our Christian walk are good predictors of how easily and naturally God will be able to guide us.

Although the parable of the ten virgins in Matthew 25:1-13 is not necessarily about guidance, it holds a powerful lesson about being

Be Ready!

I will study and get ready and then maybe the chance will come.
—Abraham Lincoln

ready and alert. Many guidance questions will come upon us suddenly, and we need to be in the same state of constant preparedness as were the five wise virgins. God requires of us that we too respond appropriately when the time comes, and that we constantly prepare for that moment.

> **Be Prepared!**
>
> Have thy tools ready. God will find thee work.
> —Charles Kingsley

25 God's Will—General and Specific

We already know plenty about God's general will, but little about His specific will—and confusing the two of them can be . . . well . . . confusing.

When Christians talk about discovering and doing God's will, they may be talking about the same thing—but sometimes not. It's important to be clear exactly what we mean when we refer to this concept, "God's will." Theologians typically distinguish between the general will of God and His specific or particular will. We need to take a look at the difference between these and what the implications of these two concepts mean for our lives.

The General Will of God

Ron Kincaid writes in *Praying for Guidance* that God's will for us is "to know Christ, to be conformed to the likeness of Christ and to share Christ."[5] This helpful summary emerges from hundreds of verses spread throughout the Bible, which together paint an overall picture of God's general will. This picture has two dimensions: the present world in which we live out our lives and the ultimate purposes that God has for His kingdom and humankind. Only the first aspect concerns us here. As we consider God's general will, we must recognize that it's the same for all people. He wants all to come to a saving knowledge of Christ. And He wants all who have made Christian commitments to live lives honoring Christ and to share the gospel message. These elements of God's general will have been the same ever since the founding of the church. In every era, in every place, God requires of Christians these qualities.

If we're honest, we seldom need much help figuring out God's general expectations of us. The guidelines for godly living are plain, embodied in such familiar

Scripture passages as the Ten Commandments or the Sermon on the Mount, and supplemented by other teachings of Jesus Himself, the apostle Paul, and so on. Equally evident, too, are the scriptural mandates for us to share the good news of Jesus Christ with all peoples.

Most of the time it's plain enough what God expects of us. The Old Testament prophet Micah provided a succinct summary of those expectations: "He has showed you, O man, what is good. And what does the LORD require of you? To act justly and to love mercy and to walk humbly with your God" (Micah 6:8). In the New Testament, Jesus provided us with a similarly distilled version of how we are to live.

> ## Your Will? Or God's?
>
> There are only two kinds of people in the end: those who say to God, "Thy will be done," and those to whom God says, "*Thy* will be done."
>
> —C. S. Lewis

Here is part of the exchange between Jesus and the lawyer who asked what he needed to do to inherit eternal life. The lawyer answered, " ' "Love the Lord your God with all your heart and with all your soul and with all your strength and with all your mind"; and, "Love your neighbor as yourself." ' 'You have answered correctly,' Jesus replied. 'Do this and you will live' " (Luke 10:27-28). No, the difficulty we have is seldom recognizing God's general will, but rather, it is **Obedience [57]** to it.

Occasionally, we find the church's thinking has been so contaminated by that of the society in which it exists that many Christians simply can't see the obvious. A simple example is how long slavery was tolerated in the United States and in the British Empire, something we now look back on with embarrassment and shame. The church has numerous other dark episodes in its history, when Christians who should have known better allowed the temptations of wealth or power to do things that must have wounded Christ deeply. For example, you might think of the Crusades, or some of the mission efforts that were as concerned with imposing Western culture on unchurched peoples as they were with taking them the gospel. God's people should always be asking how His general will applies to the church, and should always be intent on conforming to His will rather than to human culture.

Deeply committed Christians around the world today disagree on numerous social and political issues. Whether we're talking about capital punishment, dealing with poverty and the welfare system, or the potentially idolatrous nature of materialism in the Western world, Christians remain divided on how God would have us deal with major questions like these. God's deep concern for justice for all people means we should never shy away from trying to address these issues. When we work on these answers, however, we must also tend to areas where we already plainly know God's general will. If we're not serious about listening to what we do know of God's will—the more easily determined part of the picture—how can we expect Him to entrust us with details of His specific will for our individual situations?

The Specific Will of God

This area interests most of us as individuals. If we've been Christians for a while, and we're familiar with God's general expectations of us, we've read the previous few paragraphs with perhaps growing impatience. "Yes, that's all good and well," you're probably grumbling, "but where does that leave me and the need to say 'yes' or 'no' to that job offer by Friday afternoon?"

The answer to this question may not be what you want to hear. John Stott puts it bluntly: "The particular will of God will not be found in Scripture." The section on **Scripture [2]** emphasizes that God doesn't intend His Word to provide us with the detailed instructions for such decisions. That's why this section on God's Will is surrounded by 61 others, all of which emphasize the *process* by which we can discover where God is leading us in our unique situations.

We shouldn't think that God is concerned only with our seeking after His general will, and that He doesn't care about the specifics of our individual lives. **The "Abba, Father" Principle [18]** should dispel any doubts you have on that front. The point is simply that we discover God's specific will and general will in quite different ways. The section on Scripture reminds us that we always need to start with the Bible when we're seeking God's leading for our particular situation. We need to know the ground rules within which we can expect God to guide us. But we invariably need to go beyond those principles outlined in Scripture, to **Prayer [3],** seeking **Advice [4],** looking to our **Circumstances [5],** and determining whether we have a certain **Inner Peace [6]** about the entire process and the conclusion we've reached. Seeking God's specific will for our lives takes sustained effort and a patient willingness to discover His leading. Knowing God's general will is relatively easy, but difficult to live out; with His specific will, both steps can be demanding indeed. Although Paul was writing in a context that doesn't speak directly about guidance, his statement is nevertheless helpful when he said "to work out your salvation with fear and trembling, for it is God who works in you to will and to act according to his good purpose" (Philippians 2:12-13). Discovering God's specific will for our lives as we live out our salvation will take work; we are partnering with God to live lives that please Him and, as Paul put it, are "according to his good purpose."

Part of that process includes knowing the difference between God's directive will and His acceptable will. The first speaks to those things that we conclude He wants us to do. There's no arguing, negotiating, or procrastinating about it. His will is plain, and we're to go ahead and obey it. The second, His acceptable will, honors the remarkable degree of freedom He's given us. The section on **Choices, Choices [20]** makes plain that God at times allows us a wide range of alternative steps, any one of which is equally pleasing to Him. Knowing which is which is important and can be wonderfully liberating. It may be that God is saying, "My acceptable will for your life is that you can be a butcher, baker, or candlestick maker—I don't mind." God's acceptable will also is the theme of **Do What You Like [31].** (Some writers describe God's "acceptable will" as His "permissive will." The latter term is not used here, however, because it can be confused with another dimension of God's will. Sometimes His "permissive will" is used to refer to those things God doesn't want to happen, such as suffering, but which He allows to take place. What happened with Job and his many misfortunes is a good biblical example of God's permissive will.)

> ## Asking Well
>
> That which is often asked of God, is not so much his will and way, as his approval of our way.
> —Sarah F. Smiley[6]

Implications of Knowing God's Will

Once we know what God has called us to do in response either to His general or specific will, at least three implications arise:

First, there is the simple need for **Obedience [57].** Elisabeth Elliot says, "The Christian does not come to God for advice. He comes asking for God's will and . . there is no option here. Once it is known, it must be done." Our obedience, though, is not to be some grudging, reluctant sense of duty—as if we'd just learned a second cousin we don't particularly like is going to be in town and we now feel obligated to meet him for lunch. Far from an "I-suppose-I-have-to" mentality, our obedience should mirror what William Barclay describes in his commentary on the gospel of Matthew. Regarding the man who discovers a pearl of great value, who goes and sells all so he can buy the jewel (Matthew 13:45), Barclay says: "[H]owever a man discovers the will of God for himself, whether it be in the lightning flash of a moment's illumination or at the end of a long and conscious search, it is worth anything unhesitatingly to accept it."

Second, flowing from the question of obedience is the importance of how we view *our* wills. The call to obedience and faithfulness to God's will means plenty for our wills. Again, in the words of Elisabeth Elliot: "If in the integrity of my heart I speak the words, *Thy will be done,* I must be willing, if the answer requires it, that *my* will be undone. It is a prayer of commitment and relinquishment."

Third, it's crucial not to get hung up on God's will and how to find it. Mike Yaconelli underscores the dangers of becoming obsessed with God's will. He grew up, he says, having lived "under the shadow of the 'will of God'" as he felt continuous pressure to seek God's plan. He puts things in perspective when he comments, "The real issue in life is not the search for God's will, it is the search for God. The issue in faith is not knowing what God is doing, rather it is knowing that God knows what he is doing. The issue of faith is seeking God's presence, not God's plan for my life, because there is no plan outside of my knowing him. We don't need to know the will of God, we only need to know God—which is, strangely enough, his will."

Our emphasis isn't to be carrying out God's "program." It's to establish and deepen our relationship with Him. He is far more concerned with who we are and with our relationship with

> ## Where's Your Will?
>
> There are no disappointments to those whose wills are buried in the will of God.
> —Frederick William Faber

Him than He is with what we do, where we live, who we marry, or what we major in while in college. Those things are important too, but if we don't have the right relationship with God, all those other concerns become irrelevant. As John White writes in *The Fight*, "Though the Bible never uses the word *guidance*, it does talk about a Guide. You may seek guidance, but God desires to give something better: himself."

See also **The Ninety-Nine Percent Rule [26].**

26 The Ninety-Nine Percent Rule

Ninety-nine percent of the time we already know God's will, and the problem is just living it out; it's for the other one percent of the time that we need His guidance.

Christians who are serious about honoring God in their daily walk already know what to do ninety-nine percent of the time. When we go about our day-by-day tasks and routines, we don't need any direct or special guidance. We don't need to spend time in earnest prayer to know that we should show up at class or work this morning, get the kids ready for school once again, or be honest and hardworking on the job. Nor do we need any special word from the Lord to tell us to act lovingly toward our families, friends, and everyone else, or that we should be in worship on Sunday.

If we're living out our faith as we should, God's grace should be sustaining us moment by moment during our days. Having chosen to follow Christ, we've made countless other choices that we don't need to revisit. We're not free to cheat on our taxes, commit adultery, or do drugs. Those were choices we made when we became Christians. That's the ninety-nine percent part. Paul Little asks this question: "Has it ever struck you that the vast majority of the will of God for your life has already been revealed in the Bible? That is a crucial thing to grasp."[7]

Then there's the one-percent piece, those choices that command special—and sometimes excruciatingly difficult—attention. These include the major decisions of life, like career selection, choice of college, whether to marry, and whom to marry. Many other major decisions also call for this special "one-percent" guidance. It's terribly important to know which type is which. We're unlikely to move the major decisions into the routine category, but we may treat minor ones as if they belong in the major league. (See **Choices, Choices [20].**)

For the most part, the Christian life is a matter of obedience to what we already know to do—obedience to a life of discipleship that honors God. The focus of our daily lives should be on doing well what we already know is our task; we should not be obsessing over the one

percent we don't need to know anything about right now. In God's time, He'll tell us what we need. Thomas Carlyle puts it well: "Our grand business is not to see what lies dimly at a distance but to do what lies clearly at hand."

As the Introduction makes plain, this book was designed to help you think through the complexity of finding God's will in that small category of major choices we will face. So, truth be told, most of the time you won't need this book. One day you might, and that's when you don't want to be saying, "Where did I put that book about God's will?"

See also **Trivial Pursuit [27]; Unneeded Guidance [28]; Obedience [57].**

27 Trivial Pursuit

While God wants us to have warm feet, we may be insulting Him if we seek His counsel on the color of socks we should wear today.

If we're serious about living lives that please God, we *ought* to be serious about the choices and decisions we make. The trouble is, it may not always be easy to draw the line between those choices that should be brought to Him thoughtfully in prayer, such as taking a new job, and those that shouldn't, like which pair of socks to wear today or which parking space to choose. We slight God and His loving care for us if we ignore His counsel on the big decisions. Yet we may be insulting Him if we implore His wisdom and direction on things that are truly inconsequential. Far from being a mark of great piety to seek His leading on whether to choose green gift wrap or blue, doing so is a betrayal of the intelligence He's given us and reflects a deep spiritual immaturity rather than spiritual depth. Any decision that has moral or other significant implications clearly calls for us to be in touch with how God would have us act. Yet the great majority of decisions we make each day are either totally devoid of moral content (these socks or those? this parking space or that?), or else are so plainly right or wrong that we don't even have to think about them.

What's helpful here is the old picture of God having given us a watch, and the question is asked: do we honor God more by imploring Him every few minutes to tell us the time, or by simply checking the watch ourselves? Just as that answer is obvious, so too ought we avoid inconsequential decision making that makes us look like spiritual infants, utterly helpless in our ability to do even the most basic things in a normal Christian life. If you're hung up on trivia like these, it's time to move on.

28 Unneeded Guidance

Sometimes we waste our time seeking guidance when God has already shown us what we need to know.

You've probably heard the delightful tale of the fellow caught in a flood. As the waters surrounded his house and he climbed on the roof, he prayed for God to save him. When the water reached the top of the door, someone came by in a rowboat and offered him a ride. He refused the ride, because he just knew God Himself would save him. When the water reached the roof, a second rowboat arrived. Again, he refused a ride because he knew he could trust God Himself to come to his rescue. Finally, the floodwaters rose higher still, and he drowned. On arriving in heaven, he angrily asked God why He had not rescued him. God replied, "Who do you think sent you the rowboats?"

The point is sometimes we don't recognize that we already have the solutions we're asking God to give us. There are instances when we simply don't need the guidance we think we do. The work God has called us to is at hand, or the solution is so simple that we look right through it. If, for example, someone has asked you to marry him, both of you are deeply in love with each other to the extent that marriage is plainly the next step, and your friends and family all agree marriage would be an excellent move, why are you still waiting before saying "yes"? Why are you waiting for God to send you any more signals than He already has? Maybe you *have* your answer.

Sometimes (perhaps more often than we realize), the obvious answer is just that—the answer. If we keep seeking **Signs and Wonders [39],** or make guidance more complicated than it is, the rowboats will keep coming by and we're in danger of quite literally missing the boat.

See also **How God Guides [11]; Trivial Pursuit [27].**

Falling

Once you become aware that

the main business that you are here for is to know

God, most of life's problems fall into place of

their own accord.

into

J. I. Packer

Place

Making
Godly
Decisions

29 The Clarity Principle

If you can't state in one sentence the issue you're seeking guidance on, work on clarifying the destination before continuing the trip.

Usually the guidance issue or the choice before us is plain: "I accept either the offer to attend grad school in Ohio or the one to go to school in California." "We either move my wife's elderly father into a long-term care facility or we don't."

Sometimes, though, we face a problem that isn't as easily reduced to an either/or, yes/no option. Perhaps the options themselves are much more complex, or the difficulty may lie in the way we understand the problem. Quite possibly we haven't answered this question: What *exactly* is the issue on which we're seeking God's help and direction?

If you can't define your issue in one sentence, you probably need to keep thinking through what's involved. Are you in fact dealing with two (or even more) separate but related issues? Or is this one complex mess that you haven't yet adequately understood? For some of us, writing down our thoughts may help bring the clarity we need. For others, talking this through with friends or family may refine our thinking. Or simply trying to think it through, looking at it piece by piece, may be what you need. Whatever strategy you use, it's extremely important to clarify the issue to the point where you can state it simply and clearly—preferably in a single sentence.

If, despite your best efforts, you still can't do that, and the issue still seems unmanageably large or complicated, be patient. Ask God to help you clarify your thinking. In addition to **Prayer [3],** keep reading **Scripture [2]** and seeking **Advice [4]** from mature Christians or those familiar with your situation. But before you can begin **Asking the Right Questions [7]** about your issue, it's important to know what you want to ask questions *about.* If you're not there yet, the first step is to seek the guidance to clarify and refine what's at stake, thus preparing you for step two. That's when you will actually seek the guidance you're really after—but can't get until you know where you're going.

If you went to a AAA office to get some maps, but could tell the clerk only that you expect you'll need to go to the Pacific Northwest, but might need to go to Chicago or the Midwest generally, and possibly the South (but not Florida), that bewildered soul would have a tough time trying to help you. Maybe you'll end up visiting all these places, but until you have clarified the exact nature of your trip, there's little the clerk can do to help except in the most general way.

Our all-knowing God already is aware exactly what our itinerary should look like, and He's waiting to work it out with us. When we've sought His help in pointing us in the right direction, He'll also make plain the destination itself.

30 The Default Strategy

Choosing a default position by deciding to do something unless God tells you otherwise can help clarify where He's leading you.

The default strategy works well in two situations: deadlines and routines.

Deadlines

When you're heading toward a decision that has to be made, you don't want the deadline to approach while you get increasingly paralyzed because the hours and minutes are draining away and you still can't decide. With the default approach, you've already decided. But you also remain open to hearing God's word until the last minute and, if necessary, changing your mind.

So, when you're forced to make a choice between two (or more) alternatives, select a "default" option as your course of action. Then stick to it, unless in an answer to prayer or some other way, God points you to another option. What you are in effect saying is, "Lord, I don't know which way to turn on this question. Each of these paths seems equally valid. So far, You've not shown me that any option is better than another. So I'll go with number two unless I hear otherwise from You. But I remain open to Your leading; therefore, please stop me from taking this course if it's not what You want." Move ahead trusting that if God has something better in mind—and if you're honest about being open to His word—He'll show you what it is.

How About an Example?

You're asked to play a leadership role in your church's junior high group, an opportunity that you view with mixed feelings. You can make strong arguments for saying yes or no. You get no strong indication one way or another from **The Big Five [1].** The person who has asked you needs to know by noon on Sunday. It's Friday night, and you still don't know which way to turn. Choose an option, either "yes" or "no," and assume that's what you'll stick with—unless you get some clear indication to the contrary before deadline time.

Routine Situations

The default approach is also helpful in shaping your attitude toward routine situations, such as your job or ministry. At any time, God may call us from what we're doing to move into other work or ministry. But we waste vast amounts of time and spiritual energy if day by day we dwell on what He might be calling us to do next. The default mode should be, "Lord, I believe you've put me in this place to do Your work. Until I hear clearly from You that You want me to move on, I'm assuming that this is where I am to stay and I'll give it my wholehearted service and energy for You." This kind of default approach is not to be confused with a do-nothing strategy; rather, it combines an active commitment both to faithful service and openness to God's leading. (See **The Ambassador Principle [19].**)

A clear example of this from Scripture is when Paul and his companions had as their default plan a trip to Asia, but were prevented from going there by the leading of the Holy Spirit:

Paul and his companions traveled throughout the region of Phrygia and Galatia, having been kept by the Holy Spirit from preaching the word in the province of Asia.
—Acts 16:6

The "Default" Prayer

Lord, I want to do Your will in the situation facing me. I don't know which is the better choice—maybe each of the options is fine with You. I've selected one. But because I want to choose in a way that pleases You, stop me if my default mode is the wrong course. I trust that You will stop me from going astray.

See also **Godly Decision Making [36].**

31 Do What You Like

God normally calls us to tasks that fit our gifts and which we're likely to enjoy, especially when it involves our work. Assuming that we should do what we already like is a good place to begin.

In *Every Life a Plan of God*, J. Oswald Sanders describes several myths that we have about guidance. One is that "if we surrender our wills to God, he will ask us to do some difficult thing we don't want to do." Another is that "if there is something you want to do desperately, the likelihood is that God won't want you to do it." These myths can be especially crippling when we're looking at our careers. Rather than starting with the negative (and wrong) assumptions of these myths, it's much more helpful to start by imagining a conversation with God. Instead of asking God yet again what He wants you to do, imagine instead that He's asking you, "Well, what would you *like* to do?"

Many of us had parents who patiently and encouragingly supported us as we grappled with career questions. In effect, they said to us, "Do whatever you think you'll enjoy. Use your common sense, be realistic, and take some risks. Why don't you explore areas that make sense for you? We'll help you think through possibilities, and then we'll back you in any choices you make." If that's how loving and supportive parents respond, how much more encouraging and supportive is our heavenly Father likely to be?

Once we get beyond these odd misperceptions that Sanders described, we're free to do pretty well what we like. The only precondition? Seek to honor God in all that we do. If we meet that condition, we're echoing the thoughts of St. Augustine, who wrote: "Love, and do what you like." Meeting that precondition means that some career possibilities or other courses of action are off limits. The section on **Scripture [2]** notes that God has clear guidelines on what kind of thoughts, words, and deeds of ours are okay, and which aren't. Most of these things are pretty obvious, even to nonChristians who have no commitment to living a biblical lifestyle: don't murder, give help to people who need it, don't cheat or steal. Then there are others that nonChristians may see as fine, but which Scripture nevertheless explicitly forbids: premarital sex or dabbling in the occult.

The first step, therefore, should be to know what these barriers are and to recognize that as Christians we accept that God has placed limits on what's acceptable and what isn't. We need to be familiar with His constraints. Many of us do well enough on this point. But perhaps we fail to move to the second step, which points to the astonishing range of freedom that is ours within the constraints. It's as if God says to us, "You know Me well enough to understand what displeases Me; honor that, and you're then free to do whatever you like." We know, for example, that there's no way we can reconcile a Christian lifestyle with a career in drug running or peddling pornography. Those are so obviously out of keeping with what God wants that we don't need to think about it.

The Parable of the Fences

Joseph Bayly once wrote a parable about a community living on a plateau that needed to erect fences to prevent people from falling over the edge. Trouble was, some people placed the fences farther back from the edge than necessary. The result: Some risk-takers would cross a fence, only to find that nothing happened. They then concluded that the fences weren't needed—until they'd cross one that was needed as a lifesaver. The point is, if we accept the limits God has set for our own well-being—the wisely placed fences—we can concentrate on the unbounded freedom we have within them. Within those limits you can pretty well do what you like. Christians who are serious about their faith invariably find they have no desire to do things beyond the fences that are inherently displeasing to God.

We want our choices to bring us to Box 1 in the matrix below:

	Pleasing to God	Displeasing to God
Pleasing to Us	1	2
Displeasing to Us	3	4

Box 2 has us doing what we enjoy, but is plainly out of God's will. In the long term we'd find our enjoyment short-lived. Box 4 is the dumbest of places to be, as we're making both God and ourselves unhappy. Lastly, Box 3 may show us doing something that seems pleasing to God, but the fact that we're not happy about it calls for either an attitude check on our part, or the need for us to do something else—something that moves us back to Box 1 and pleases both Him and us. That ideal, as indicated throughout the Psalms, is exactly what He has in mind.

See also **The Scrooge Pitfall [55].**

32 Excuses, Excuses

Don't avoid God's call with excuses and false humility; His harshest answer to you is that He may ask someone else to do His work.

When we think how much we're inclined to make excuses in our Christian lives, there's much comfort in knowing that God has used people who seemed superbly gifted in this area. For example, the account of God calling Moses to lead the children of Israel out of Egypt is almost comical in the way Moses desperately seeks to avoid the work God has in store for him. Read Exodus 3 to see the growing desperation and increasing honesty of his excuses as Moses seeks to avoid this divine call. Even though there was no mistaking that this was God Himself speaking to him, Moses can at a moment's notice come up with one excuse after another why God should turn to someone else. Or, at the very least, just leave him alone.

Fortunately, Moses learns that excuses are no match for the living God—and it's a lesson he learns in time. One of the realities of God's kingdom is that He will accomplish His plans and His purposes, with or without us. Ian McLaren warns us that "It is an awful condemnation for a man to be brought by God's providence face to face with a great possibility of service and blessing, and then to show himself such that God has to put him aside, and look for other instruments."[1]

> ## Simple Obedience
>
> God has given his order: that is an end of it. There is no need for argument.
> —James S. Stewart[2]

33 Fleeces

Using Gideon's strategy of laying out a fleece isn't necessarily a bad idea, but it isn't a particularly good one either.

In Judges 6 we read the story of Gideon using a fleece on two occasions to confirm what God had already told him to do: Lead the Israelites into battle against the Midianites. First, he lays out a wool fleece on the threshing floor and tells God that if there's dew only on the fleece the next morning, and not on the surrounding ground, "then I will know that you will save Israel by my hand, as you said" (verse 37). God does just this, and the next morning Gideon discovers a fleece so wet that he can squeeze a bowlful of water out if it. Then Gideon realizes that one might expect that a heavy dew on the fleece would not evaporate as quickly, and that perhaps his test isn't as reassuring as he hoped. So he ups the ante and asks instead for something remarkable: for the ground to be wet, while the fleece is dry. So, with due reverence and an acute awareness that he's testing God's patience, he says: "Do not be angry with me. Let me make just one more request. Allow me one more test with the fleece. This time make the fleece dry and the ground covered with dew" (verse 39).

You probably recall the outcome, as God indulges a man who saw himself as hopelessly unfit for the work to which God called him. More than anything, Gideon sought assurance, a sign, that it was God Himself from whom he would be taking his orders, and in whose promise of victory he could have complete confidence.

Gideon's wonderfully human story provides a rich case study in guidance. Many of us can relate to his insecurities, if not his experience of direct encounters with an angel or God's supernatural intervention at Gideon's request. Several lessons emerge from this story, including the reality that if God wants to get our attention, or get His word to us, He'll find a way to do so. Our concern here is with the more focused question of Gideon's use of a fleece. Should we use a comparable approach in seeking God's leading in our lives?

The short answer is, "probably not." Some take a firm stand against such approaches. J. Oswald Sanders, for instance, writes: "Outward signs such as Gideon's fleece, far from being evidence of superior spirituality, are in reality a concession to feeble faith." In similar vein, M. Blaine Smith says, "The New Testament demonstrates that the Spirit-filled believer has all the inner resources necessary for sound decision making." He adds that using a fleece approach to guidance represents an abdication of personal responsibility because "it usually amounts to an effort to shortcut a decision, to reduce the thinking and risk involved." In other words, spiritually mature people don't stoop to such silly techniques.

And yet it's easy to have sympathy for Gideon, who is minding his own business trying to avoid the attention of the Midianites, secretly threshing wheat in a winepress, when an angel appears. The angel greets this most unlikely leader by telling him, "The Lord is with you, mighty warrior"—an ironic statement given his lack of boldness! Then begins what is probably the most intensive bout of spiritual arm wrestling recorded in Scripture since Moses tried to resist God's call to him in the wilderness. As the story unfolds we see an increasingly emboldened leader. We read in Judges 6:34 that "the Spirit of the LORD came upon Gideon," who summons the Israelites to rally against the Midianites.

That's when his nerve fails him. Suddenly, it seems, he realizes what he's gotten himself into: Who is he, the least in his family, from the weakest clan in his tribe, presuming to lead the nation into battle? Despite Gideon's encounters with angels, despite his experience with the Spirit of the Lord, can any of us blame him for calling a timeout? It's at this point that he desperately turns to **Signs and Wonders [39]** for assurance. In addition, as John White points out, "Gideon had far fewer resources when it came to knowing God's will than we have. He had probably never seen a copy of the books of Moses or the book of Joshua. He may not even have been aware of how God led his people out of Egypt. His home was a center of idolatry. We, on the other hand, have the whole range of Scripture open to us and the constant illumination of the Holy Spirit."

Did Gideon act in a way that we would now define as spiritually immature? Yes. But another important lesson here is that God meets us where we are, just as He did Gideon. What's important about Gideon is that he was ready to do God's bidding, but he desperately wanted to be sure that he hadn't somehow gotten horribly crossed signals, and that it was *him* to whom God had appointed this task, not the

Gideon in the next village. His **Doubts [48]**, fears, and deep insecurity are understandable. Yet when God has humored this man, he becomes the "mighty warrior" who defeats the Midianites.

While God meets us where we are, He doesn't want to leave us there. God moves Gideon beyond the fleece exercises to making him a true hero of the faith. With his bold reliance on God alone, he utterly disregards all military common sense by defeating the enemy exactly as he's been ordered. What Gideon did was seek a sign to confirm something he had already been plainly told to do. While that was understandable, his action still reflected weak rather than deep faith, and exposed him to the various problems associated with "seeking after signs."

Are we then never to use anything comparable to the kind of request that Gideon placed before the Lord? M. Blaine Smith offers some helpful thinking in this regard: "God may sometimes honor a fleece which is put out in sincerity, especially by a young believer who is not in a position to know better." As we've seen with Gideon, God does at times work this way. But we need to be wary of some difficulties inherent in this approach.

The Problem with Fleeces

At its worst, using a fleece is no different from **Flipping a Coin [34]** in a mindlessness that comes awfully close to a pagan-like superstition. For example, you're not sure whether to take that significant promotion at work, which entails an even mix of pluses and minuses. So you ask God to show you clearly what He wants, and that if the next person who phones you at work is female, you'll take the job, and if it's a male caller, you won't. You'll get a clear answer, once the phone rings. But what kind of basis is this for making any decision, let alone a major one? As noted above, this approach trivializes the far more sensible ways God has given us for discerning His will.

At its best, using a fleece can still be marked with problems, where we in effect "put God on the spot" as we try to force from Him an answer that He perhaps isn't ready or willing to give us. Trying to force the Lord's hand is never a smart move. Even if we are acting with the sincerest of motives, using a fleece means we're not carefully thinking through the issues that deserve our attention. Therefore, it's helpful to pause a moment and ask why we're wanting to use the fleecing tactic. Is it that we lack assurance for what we think God has told us to do? Or that we want a decision in a hurry? Or that we have a tough choice between A and B, and cannot easily decide which way to go? Each of these circumstances might move us toward pursuing the fleece option. Yet for each of these situations there also is a more thoughtful approach, and one that is probably more pleasing to God. (See **The Default Strategy [30]; Guidance in a Crunch [37]; Courage [47]**.)

Can God use a fleecing approach to guide us? Of course. Will He? Probably not. And is this one of His preferred methods for helping us make godly decisions? The consensus of Christians is a clear "no." The reason lies partly in how God has chosen to work differently with Christians, who since Pentecost have the working of the Holy Spirit in their lives. In the Old Testament, we see numerous examples of the fleece/lot casting/seeking-after-signs approach to knowing God's will. Yet in the New Testament, we see that the church operates differently. Here's a final word from M. Blaine Smith: "[A]fter the day of Pentecost there is no further instance in Scripture of casting lots. Nor is there any example of an approach to God's will akin to putting out a fleece. This suggests to me that after this time the practice was no longer necessary."

God may well have guided you in the past using a fleece. If so, the reasons listed here

> **Resource**
>
> For an excellent, comprehensive discussion on this topic, read *Knowing God's Will*, by M. Blaine Smith, chapter 13.
>
> See also **How God Guides [11]; Maturity [14]; Testing, Testing [16]; Signs and Wonders [39]**.

suggest that this kind of guidance probably best belongs in the past, in the child-hood of your faith, and not in the maturing future to which God is calling you.

34 Flipping a Coin

While there's biblical precedent for this kind of decision making in guidance, at best it's a last resort—and definitely tough to imagine Jesus doing.

Sometimes you need to choose between two options that you think would be equally acceptable to God, but you've exhausted all other ways of trying to distin-guish between these possibilities and see no advantage of selecting one over the other. Flipping a coin can make your decision for you. That is neither a particularly thoughtful or spiritual approach. If anything, coin flipping smacks of abdicating our responsibility to make God-shaped decisions, and reflects instead a mindlessness that's far removed from the more thoughtful, Spirit-led approaches that God typi-cally expects us to bring to guidance.

Can God use this approach? Certainly; after all, He used Balaam's ass to speak His word. To be fair, we find elsewhere in the Old Testament examples of casting lots, which are essentially a coin flipping approach to godly decision making. (See Exodus 28:29-31 on the Urim and Thummim.) In the New Testament, too, we have a precedent for casting lots, with the selection of Matthias to succeed Judas Iscariot as one of the apostles (Acts 1:26). But is that the most appropriate approach to mak-ing choices if you've prayed for and expect the Holy Spirit's leading in your deci-sion making? Derek Tidball, writing in *How Does God Guide?*, says it seems significant that "we never read of the early Church using the drawing of lots again to find out God's will. From the Day of Pentecost on they seem to have operated on a differ-ent basis. Urim and Thummim guidance was mechanical. With the giving of the Holy Spirit there was no longer any need to resort to these external means of guid-ance since he was within and among his people."[3]

For example, we have no instances of Paul flipping coins or drawing lots. He seemed always to rely on the leading of the Holy Spirit and the good sense God had given him. And it's tough to imagine Jesus sighing, "Well, I guess I could go either way on this one; anyone have a denarius you could lend me?"

To paraphrase Paul's words from his introduction to 1 Corinthians 13, God wants to "show us a more excellent way" (1 Corinthians 12:31).

See also **Maturity [14]; The Default Strategy [30]; Fleeces [33].**

35 Formation Flying

The Christian life isn't a solo enterprise; God guides us in keeping with His will for the church and His kingdom.

This simple point is easily neglected in our highly individualistic culture. Richard Foster comments in *Celebration of Discipline* that "Perhaps our preoccupation with private guidance is the product of our Western individualism. The people of God have not always been so."

If we undervalue or disregard our role in the church and God's kingdom, we're in danger of making two possible mistakes. One is that we make decisions that leave us playing less of a part in the body of Christ than we should. The other is that we don't take advantage of the church's support in coming to a decision. By flying solo, we're acting unbiblically and we forfeit the benefit of advice or prayer support from our local church, or the possibility of mature Christians confirming our sense of call to a particular ministry.

Foster gives several examples of how the local church helps us make godly decisions. One concerns a couple who, believing that God was leading them to be married, wanted "the confirmation of a Spirit-directed body"—which they received.

If you're relatively new to your local church, maybe you haven't yet developed the relationships needed for the vulnerable conversations you might seek. In that case, check in with people from your previous church or with other Christians you trust. Maybe you

> ## The Wisdom of the Church
>
> Do not neglect the wisdom of the church. It was designed by God specifically to assist people who need wise counsel, and he uses the church as one of the tools for shaping our lives.
>
> —Bruce Waltke[4]

need to look beyond the local fellowship to the broader church for direction on formation flying.

In summary: God has placed us in His church for good reason—and it's well worth remembering this when it comes to questions of guidance and seeking His will for our individual lives.

See also **Advice [4]**.

> **The Experience of the Church**
>
> The long experience of the church is more likely to lead to correct answers than is the experience of the lone individual.
>
> —Elton Trueblood

36 Godly Decision Making

Anyone can make decisions; what God expects of us are decisions that are made with Him and His kingdom in mind.

Godly decision making consists of two parts: the careful decision making that befits responsible members of God's family, as well as a spiritual dimension that uniquely equips us to act in accordance with God's will for our lives. How are we to blend these two qualities as we seek to make a decision? Here are ten questions to help attain that goal:

Ten Questions for Making Godly Decisions

- What exactly needs to be decided? Can you summarize the need in one sentence? Thinking it through in writing will be extremely helpful in clarifying exactly what the issue is. (See **The Clarity Principle [29]**.)
- What additional information do you need to make this decision?
- How will you know when you have enough information to decide? Or will you just keep gathering more data? Sometimes your options are clear enough, but involve extremely difficult calls between two closely balanced

alternatives. On other occasions, you don't yet know enough to reach a decision. Be prepared at times to live with the reality that you simply won't be able to gather as much information as you'd like, but still you must decide. (See **Guidance in a Crunch [37]; Indecision [52].**)

- What criteria will be important in making your decision? To what extent do those criteria explicitly take God into account? It's been said that "To judge a thing, one must first know the standard." By what standards will you make your decision? If you're not clear on these, how will you know whether you've decided well? Management consultant John D. Arnold says in selecting criteria for decision making, it's important to identify standards that will help you determine what you want to achieve with your decision, what you want to preserve, and what you want to avoid.[5]

- On which of these criteria can you be flexible? Which of these are non-negotiable? Establish priorities among your criteria. Thus, in deciding on a new job, you can probably flex on salary and benefits, but maybe excessive travel time that would take you away from your family is something you see as nonnegotiable.

- Is this decision likely to honor God? Or will it at least avoid bringing Him dishonor?

- What steps have you taken to counter your own selfish interests as you explore this decision? (See **Ambition [43]; Mixed Motives [54].**)

- What kind of choice is involved here? Is it between two or more options, each of which would be acceptable to God? How much freedom do you have in making this choice? (See **Choices, Choices [20]; God's Will [25].**)

- What values underlie this decision? Always there are values in tension in making a decision, otherwise there'd be nothing for you to decide. Can you identify these values? Is there any single value that overrides all others? Is there any one principle, that of honesty, for example, that emerges as most important? If so, does that realization make your decision for you?

- To whom do you owe loyalty in making this decision? Presumably, you seek to honor God in this decision, but who else is a stakeholder in this decision?

The very nature of decision making involves choosing one course of action from two or more competing options. The most difficult decisions are those in which the options seem so well balanced in their pluses and minuses that you don't know which way to turn. One option here might be to turn to **The Default Strategy [30]**. Another might be to use the trick employed by Sigmund Freud, which John White describes in his book, *The Fight*. When Freud faced a tough choice, he told friends he'd flip a coin. "To their astonished inquiries," White writes, "he replied, 'If when the coin comes down I am pleased, then I know what it was I *really* wanted. If on the other hand I am disappointed, I am clearer as to what I *don't want* to do.'"

Forcing ourselves to respond to the reactions that Freud's technique generates helps us clarify our thinking, motives, and fears. Throughout the decision making process, as we gain new insights like these, we can bring before God a richer, more informed background as we continue to ask Him to help us shape our choice.

See also **Asking The Right Questions [7]; Clear Thinking [9]**.

Pilgrimage to Wholeness

Good decision making is not a mindless emotional reaction. It is a Spirit-controlled, clear-thinking process, part of our pilgrimage to wholeness.

—Gloria Gaither

Decisions Without Fanfare

No trumpets sound when the important decisions of our life are made.

—Agnes de Mille

For Better or for Worse

Good decisions get better, bad ones get worse.

—Unknown

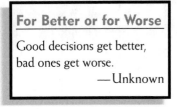

37 Guidance in a Crunch

When you have to make a choice quickly, remember that here too the guidance seeking principles remain the same: go back to the basics of **The Big Five [1]**.

Your three-year-old daughter is desperately ill, and the doctor outlines two possible treatments, each of them high risk. While you feel as well informed as you can be on the facts, you simply don't know which way to go. The decision is yours, and you know it has to be made almost immediately if the physician is to have a chance of saving your daughter's life.

Without warning, you sometimes find yourself needing to make a major decision—and an answer is needed in the next eight minutes, the next two hours, or perhaps the next day. Buying more time simply isn't an option. Always, even in circumstances like these, you want to return to The Big Five as your starting point. In this example, you're not going to find anything specific in Scripture to point you to the preferred treatment. The general will of God is that three-year-old daughters are healthy and well, but the Bible will say nothing about which of two medical procedures is the better option. You will, undoubtedly, be seeking whatever leading you can get from the fragmented prayers you interject into the medical drama that's unfolding before you. But, if we're honest, few of us would be able to engage in meaningful, answer-seeking prayer under those conditions. As for advice, what the doctor has outlined is all you can draw upon; there is simply no time to get second opinions. The circumstances are stark and simple—and knowing the stakes that come with your choice, you're unlikely to have inner peace about *either* option you select.

We're assuming here that you in fact have time to make something resembling a considered choice. The very nature of a choice means that you have at least some time to weigh two or more alternative options. The shorter the timeframe for any consideration, the closer you're moving away from a genuine decision to what is increasingly becoming reflexive behavior. If you're standing at a busy intersection waiting for the traffic to stop, and a stranger next to you begins to step in the path of an oncoming car, you're likely to grab his arm and pull him back. That's the kind of immediate response that allows no time to consider your moral obligations as a fellow human being to save him from harm. This isn't a situation where you exercised a genuine choice. Instead, it was an impulsive act, flowing from minimal thought. As we have more time to consider our options, we can seek God's guidance to fill in for the instinctive, reflexive actions on which, fortunately, we need to rely only rarely in ordinary life.

Therefore, an important question is, "Just how much time do we have available to think through this choice?" It may be that grim though our circumstances are, we're not facing the deadline that we thought we were. Perhaps the situation *does* in fact allow us more time than we realized. The life and death examples mentioned here of the three-year-old daughter and the pedestrian stranger are rare. Usually, even when we're facing intense pressure to act, it's worth asking the question: Is the "deadline" I see emerging coming from *my* interpretation of the situation, or would it also be *God's* interpretation?

What we see as a call for immediate action—that a deadline is upon us—may not always be how God sees things. **Waiting [40]** for God to lead us is almost always the wiser course. At times we do face true, unmovable deadlines. When we do, we must act as best we are able, and simply trust the outcome to God. But it's also helpful to look again at our situation to see if we're facing a true deadline—or a case of understandable but potentially dangerous impatience that could grow into full-blown disobedience.

Two Old Testament examples are worth noting. The first concerns King Saul and the crisis described in 1 Samuel 13. Facing an attack from the Philistines, and in charge of troops who "were quaking with fear," Saul awaited Samuel's arrival. Finally, with troops beginning to desert, Saul decided he could wait no longer and went ahead and made the burnt offering that Samuel should have given. In verse 11, Samuel asked, "What have you done?" After hearing Saul's explanation that he felt compelled to make the offering intended to secure the Lord's favor, Samuel condemned his king's impatience—and pronounced the end of Saul's kingdom. To us, this may seem an unduly harsh judgment; after all, as king, Saul was facing a major military crisis. Surely his actions were not that unreasonable. Just how much longer could he be expected to wait, anyway? But that's not how God, and his servant Samuel, saw things. Saul knew what God expected of him—even in a time of crisis. It cost him his

Crunch Time

Everyone says we must do something; and, indeed, things seem to have reached so desperate a pitch that we must. Behind are the Egyptians; right and left are inaccessible precipices; before is the sea. It is not easy at such times to stand still and see the salvation of God; but we must.

—F. B. Meyer

kingdom when he disobeyed because he saw a deadline crying for action.

So what help is The Big Five under conditions like these? Flawed though they may seem at a time like this, they are still our foundation for guidance. It may be that in turning to this five-point checklist in our minds, we will somehow hear God's leading or voice. Let us never forget that in moments of intense crisis like this, He is still guiding and leading us. He has not left us alone. Therefore, as the deadline for our decision comes upon us, it may be that the most important thing we can do is recall that God is beside us, ready even in the chaos to guide us. Perhaps all we can do is quickly commit to God whichever step presents itself to us as the better option, for whatever reason. If you can't decide, or are so overwhelmed by the implications of a choice you feel ill equipped to make, then choose either option. We can be confident at the very least that there was no indication our choice was displeasing to God; He knows all too well the limits and the circumstances under which we sometimes must make decisions. Remember too His character of a loving Father, who is aching with us as we watch our child in the imminent grasp of death.

Let's take comfort from the fact that even in moments of intense deadline decision making, God is still with us. Our lives, and everything about our futures and us, are in His hands. While it's hard to imagine under these circumstances the ramifications should we make what is a "wrong" choice, but even if we did, we serve a God who could trump what we had done—and steer things exactly as He wants them to go.

See also **Getting Ready for Guidance [24]; Godly Decision Making [36]; "Wit's End" Guidance [42]**.

38 The "Pain and Problems" Principle

We're more open to guidance when things are going badly in our lives.

W. T. Purkiser says, "God does not offer us a way out of the testings of life. He offers us a way through, and that makes all the difference."[6] The way through the trials of life is made up of guidance and grace, with guidance showing us the direction to go and grace giving us the spiritual energy to keep moving forward. An additional part of this picture is that we're far more inclined to turn to God in the first place when we have major needs. When we face the serious illness of a loved one, a major legal problem, or the loss of a job, we may suddenly find ourselves depending on God in ways we had not done before, both for His guidance and His grace.

Precisely because we're far more likely to turn to God in troubled times, we need to be aware that the nature of our problems may cloud our thinking. Yes, we're more open than ever to what God wants us to do, but will we even hear His voice in the storm we're facing? It's helpful to keep in mind the need for careful **Listening [13]**; also, some thoughts on "**Wit's End" Guidance [42]** may be helpful.

> ### A Prayer for Help
>
> Dear God: Help me get up. I can fall down by myself.
>
> —Jewish saying

In addition, we should ask ourselves, Do we really want to wait until a crisis befalls us before getting the practice we should in seeking God's leading in our lives? A healthy, ongoing relationship in our lives with family members and close friends means we can far more easily turn to them in times of great need. None of us takes kindly to family or friends who are in touch only when they have a problem.

God also seeks a continuous relationship with us. While He promises to help us in times of trouble, are we in danger of cheating ourselves of a day-by-day relationship with Him by turning to Him only at those moments? Do we tend to see God as some kind of divine concierge at Holy Living Hotel, who'll step in and help us whenever we have a problem—but is essentially irrelevant to our lives the rest of the time?

See also **Getting Ready for Guidance [24]**.

39 Signs and Wonders

God normally works in ordinary ways to tell us what He wants us to know; seeking the extraordinary reflects our lack of faith, not its depth.

Scripture refers to a wide range of ways in which God guides or otherwise communicates with His people. Some fall in the extraordinary category. In the Old Testament, we have examples of Joseph and his dreams, the burning bush by which God arrested Moses' attention, the wet and dry fleece phenomenon He worked for

Gideon, and Isaiah's vision that culminates with his profound readiness to serve: "Here am I. Send me!" (Isaiah 6:8). In the New Testament, examples include a combination of dreams and angels in God's communication with both Mary and Joseph concerning Jesus' birth, Jesus Himself appearing miraculously after His resurrection to give His disciples His charge for the work that lay ahead, and Peter's release from

> **Searching for a Miracle?**
>
> Guard against anticipating or searching for miracles to find God's will. You don't need them.
>
> —Charles R. Swindoll

prison by an angel so that he could continue his preaching ministry.

In each instance, we have a direct, miraculous intervention in the lives of God's people, sometimes when they were quietly minding their own business, sometimes when they were desperately seeking some word or leading from Him. Yet regardless of the circumstances associated with these examples, and numerous others that we could cite, several principles emerge for our understanding of guidance:

1. God chooses how He will speak to us; we don't determine that.
2. Such instances of extraordinary guidance are highly exceptional.
3. For those to whom God's word comes in such extraordinary ways, there's no doubt about the source of the message.

The implication for us? We make a huge mistake if we expect God's response to our prayers for guidance to be a "signs and wonders" answer. The section titled **How God Guides [11]** emphasizes that God almost always will use ordinary means to convey His will to us. For those rare occasions when, for whatever reason, He deems special means are called for, He will use them. F. B. Meyer writes that "When Peter was shut up in prison . . . an angel was sent to do for him what he could not do for himself; but when they had passed through a street or two of the city, the angel left him to consider the matter for himself." And that's the way God continues to deal with us, says Meyer. If miraculous intervention is needed, God will provide it. Almost all the time, however, it isn't.

If we're tempted to look for any signs and wonders in the guidance strategy God may use with us, we may also be likely to put a self-deceiving value on the importance of coincidences. Perhaps you're unsure whether you should go on a summer mission trip to Mexico. Then, the day before you need to decide, you happen to see a short TV news story about Mexico, a friend mentions that he had lunch at a new Mexican restaurant in town, and you notice the woman in front of you in the supermarket checkout line is speaking Spanish. Is this God's way of telling you to go on the trip? Or is this simply a sequence of totally random occurrences that have absolutely nothing to do with your decision? The answer is pretty clear. There's no indication whatever that these totally unrelated incidents speak to your situation. You can safely assume that God can, and will, do better than this in pointing His way. For one thing, have you ever noticed how you can "make your own coincidences happen"? If you're thinking of buying a new computer but are unsure if this is a wise move, don't be surprised if you start noticing more computer ads in the media. Is this God's way of telling you to go ahead and buy one? Probably not. You'd need something more substantial and thoughtful to arrive at a sound decision. Coincidences may be a sign. But more likely, they're nothing more than an unrelated string of events that provide the flimsiest of foundations for making major decisions.

Derek Tidball on Being Guided by Signs . . .

[The use of signs] does not seem to come highly recommended as a method of finding guidance. It is not really difficult to understand why. Honesty compels us to admit that you can usually find the sign you are looking for; that signs can be read several ways at once; that our minds play tricks on us; and that such signs often trivialize profound issues and vice versa.[7]

Of course, we shouldn't say that God will *never* use the supernatural or the extraordinary to direct us. There may be times when He might not otherwise easily get our attention, or perhaps wants to leave us in no doubt whatever that He has spoken. Think for example of how the apostle Paul could always turn to the life-changing, miraculous intervention of God on the road to Damascus. If ever Paul had second thoughts about his faith, he just had to recall that experience to reaffirm the reality and power of God in his life.

Demanding a Miracle?

Faith accepts quiet guidance. Only unbelief demands a miracle.

—Unknown

As a general rule, though, few Christians receive such stunning divine leading. Nor should we seek it. Far from longing for the presence of "signs and wonders" in our guidance because it will indicate how spiritual we are, it might reveal exactly the opposite: that we're so spiritually deaf that God cannot reach us through normal channels, and had to resort to extra measures to get through. So, we should resist our secret desires that say, "Lord, please send me some spectacular wonder work that will leave me in no doubt that it's You speaking." Instead of a sign or wonder, His response might be: "Tell me first why you think you deserve miracle-level attention."

40 Waiting

Waiting for God's leading is extraordinarily difficult, unnatural—and always worthwhile.

John Stott on Waiting . . .

It is a mistake to be in a hurry or grow impatient with God. It took him about 2,500 years to fulfill his promises to Abraham in the birth of Christ. It took him eighty years to prepare Moses for his life work. It takes him about twenty-five years to make a mature human being. So then, if we *have* to make a decision by a certain deadline, we must make it. But if not, and the way forward is still uncertain, it is wiser to wait.

Let's be honest: Waiting for God's leading is one of the most difficult aspects of guidance. Whether we're under growing pressure from others to make a decision, or we ourselves simply want closure and to know what steps to take next, our natural impatience can make waiting the last thing we want to do. But wait we must. Christians throughout the ages have learned that we dare not rush God; He works according to His timetable, and if we're serious about seeking His purposes in our lives, we need to fit in with His way of doing things.

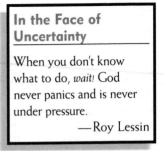

In the Face of Uncertainty

When you don't know what to do, *wait!* God never panics and is never under pressure.

—Roy Lessin

Not all decisions are of equal importance, as we saw in **Choices, Choices [20].** Some are clear enough that they can be decided without much or any waiting. Here, however, we're talking about those choices that do require waiting—either because we need to do more processing and thinking, or because we're simply waiting for God to act.

Sometimes it's best to decide by using **The Default Strategy [30],** where we say we'll decide one way or another by a certain time. Or we might be facing a tight deadline when we have to decide in a hurry. Most often, though, the problem is simply our impatience. We *want* to decide soon, largely because we want to *know* which way we'll be heading. Like children on a long car trip, we keep asking Mom or Dad, "When will we be there? How much longer?" It seems moms and dads always give the same kind of vague answers that we get from God: "Soon" or "A little while yet." Yet, as we know from the car rides of our childhood, we do eventually reach our destinations. The problem was never really whether we'd find out where we were going, as much as it was our impatience on the journey.

How Long Must I Wait?

How long, O LORD? Will you forget me forever? How long will you hide your face from me? How long must I wrestle with my thoughts and every day have sorrow in my heart?

—Psalm 13:1-2

We may be in waiting mode for several reasons. One is that God simply isn't ready to tell us what the next step is to be. Maybe He's putting various

Wait Patiently— Jesus Will Act

More mistakes are probably made by speed than by sloth, by impatience than by dilatoriness. God's purposes often ripen slowly. If the door is shut, don't put your shoulder to it. Wait till Christ takes out the key and opens it.

—John Stott

things in place before He can show us what to do or where to go. A second reason is that perhaps we need more time to think through a decision, and God is wisely holding back giving us any sense of peace or clear assurance until we've done that. Sometimes a decision may be so complex that it needs time to percolate or mature, and we'd be foolish to move to an early judgment. Other times, the reason for waiting may be a mystery. We simply can't see why God seems to have put our pleas for guidance in a "Call Waiting" queue. Whatever the reason, the waiting is difficult indeed.

One thing that may help is that we should not see waiting as a time of pathetic helplessness, when we sit wringing our hands and feeling sorry for ourselves. Eugene Peterson points out that waiting "is not fatalistic resignation. It means going about our assigned tasks, confident that God will provide the meaning and the conclusions. . . . It is the opposite of desperate and panicky manipulations, of scurrying and worrying." We ought to see this waiting mode as a time of growth and spiritual stretching—not a time when our spiritual lives are in some kind of limbo. What is it we can learn about our Christian walk during the days, weeks, months, or perhaps even years of waiting? While we may accept in theory that the waiting will end, an important question is, "How will God evaluate the way we handled this time? Will we come through this time with patience and a quiet reliance on Him? Or will it be with an attitude of checking our watches every few minutes and an irritation that signals our displeasure with how God is going about His business?"

See also **Indecision [52].**

Why Wait?

We must wait for God, long, meekly, in the wind and wet, in the thunder and lightning, in the cold and dark. Wait, and he will come. He never comes to those who do not wait.

—Frederick William Faber

41 What Would Jesus Do?

What better question to ask if we want to be like Him?

This question has helped countless Christians grapple their way through tough problems. Popularized by Charles Sheldon in the book, *In His Steps*, the question has a powerful simplicity in getting to the heart of how one should model Christ in any given situation. The question is extremely helpful in reminding us of general guidelines for Christlike conduct. Because we're called to imitate Christ, asking "What would Jesus do?" should increasingly come as second nature as we grow in our faith.

We abuse this tool if we try using it to seek highly specific answers. We can easily slip away from **Asking the Right Questions [7].** On one hand, if we ask how Jesus would handle the difficult situation we face with our boss, we'll be reminded of the Christlike principles we need to bring to a tense meeting. But if we ask what color wallpaper Jesus might choose for our family room, we don't need divine guidance as much as an interior decorator.

See also **Trivial Pursuit [27].**

42 "Wit's End" Guidance

When you're on the edge of despair and have no sense whatsoever which direction to pursue, clinging to God's grace will suffice until you can once again think about thinking, guidance, and deciding.

Sometimes we hit rock-bottom. Either through a sudden catastrophe in our lives (like the death of a loved one), a steady erosion of our spiritual vitality, or some other cause, we find ourselves running on empty. Your head may still believe, but your heart and spirit are totally wrung out, perhaps to the point of lifelessness.

Maybe we know we're experiencing a temporary spiritual systems crash, and that, as we've done before, we'll come out of it soon enough. Or we could be in a chronic season of spiritual gloom that's already lasted months or even years. Richard Foster says that "[I]t is quite possible to fear, obey, trust and rely upon the Lord and still 'walk in darkness and have no light' [Isaiah 50:10]. You are living in obedience but have entered a dark night of the soul." He's describing what many Christians have written about over the centuries, a condition marked by "a sense of dryness, depression, even lostness," says Foster.

Alternatively, our spiritual health may generally be in good shape but we're on the verge of despair, having wrestled long and hard with a problem that seems incapable of being solved. It may be a child who's using drugs, conflicts at work or home, or health difficulties that should have been resolved by now but aren't. You're at your wit's end, not knowing what to do next.

Regardless of what has brought you to where you are, important decisions still may demand attention. Yet you may be so spiritually numb that trying to make godly decisions seems as irrelevant to you as a gourmet meal is to someone with a vicious bout of flu. What do you do at moments like these? Your situation parallels those described in **Guidance in a Crunch [37],** although here you have the added difficulty of being psychologically and emotionally far less able to work through guidance issues.

One important reality to cling to at times like these is knowing that our lives are completely in God's hands. Nothing can befall us without God's knowledge and consent; nor will He allow our circumstances to override His plans for our well-being. It's not as if He says, "Well, too bad that car wreck you were in left you in no shape to think carefully about taking that job in California; you made the wrong call and you're now doomed to live in the shadow of that blunder forever." Instead, we do well to recall Romans 8:28: "And we know that in all things God works for the good of those who love him, who have been called according to his purpose." God simply won't let our incapacity at the time we should be deciding wisely count against us.

A second reality to cling to is that His grace is available to sustain us during the most difficult of moments. As Oswald Chambers says,

> ## Power in Weakness
>
> About this thing, I have pleaded with the Lord three times for it to leave me, but he has said, "My grace is enough for you: my power is at its best in weakness."
>
> —2 Corinthians 12:8-9 (JB)

"God never gives strength for tomorrow, or for the next hour, but only for the strain of the minute." We're therefore not to worry about six months down the road, next week, or even tomorrow. Jesus Himself told us, "So do not be anxious about tomorrow; tomorrow will look after itself" (Matthew 6:34, REV). At these dark times we may need to turn to those especially able to help us: family, friends, our church community, or perhaps professionals who are specifically trained to address the problems we face—a lawyer, doctor, pastor, or counselor. With the combination of care and competence these support people can bring, they can steer you toward the decisions you need to make—or in extreme cases, even make them for you.

While these are the worst of times for any decision making, especially major ones, you want to defer any decisions you can. But when you can't, go ahead anyway, drawing upon whatever human support you can—and then hand over your situation to God knowing you and your needs cannot be in better hands.

See also **Advice [4]; Change [8]; Guidance in a Crunch [37]; Worry [56].**

Admirable Faith

It is at night that faith in light is admirable.
        —Edmond Rostand

Never allow the thought, "I am of no use where I am." You certainly can be of no use where you are not.

Oswald Chambers

Being Used by God

Understanding Calling and Ambition

Do nothing out of selfish ambition or vain conceit, but in humility consider others better than yourselves.

Philippians 2:3

43 Ambition — An Uneasy Path

Few of us succeed in balancing our desires for advancement and success while letting God have His way; ambition in life is packed with potential for deluding ourselves about God's will.

Luke 9:46 tells us that "An argument started among the disciples as to which of them would be the greatest." Jesus' response to their dispute is enlightening. Curiously, He didn't condemn their quest for greatness. Instead, "knowing their thoughts," He in effect said to them, "Depends on what you mean by greatness. Let me give you *my* definition." He pointed to a small child and said, "[H]e who is least among you all — he is the greatest." In other words, He turns the disciples' assumptions about greatness upside down.

Today, too, Jesus turns our assumptions about greatness and ambition upside down. When we ask questions about our lives, and if our ambitions are acceptable to Him, He replies, "Of course be ambitious — but it depends what you mean by ambition." Figuring out the role of ambition in our lives is like doing a circus high wire act. Leaning too far one way, we fall — to the temptation of pride, self-aggrandizement, and a short-sighted advancement of our fortunes that in the long-term seriously can harm our spiritual well-being. If we lean too far in the opposite direction, we also fall —

to a false pride or unwarranted inferiority that leads to a life lived below the potential and promise God has for us. How do we attain that balance between seeking our selfish interests and putting a brake on who and what God wants us to become?

The section on **Hubris [51]** notes that humility is a proper estimation of oneself: a healthy, God-shaped understanding of both our gifts and potential for His service, as well as the limitations we bring.

As we seek His guidance, we can be sure God wants our lives to reflect this balance. As we try that, we should look at how Jesus forced His disciples to think through what they meant by "greatness." He forces us to ask the right questions. Asking "Should Christians be ambitious?" is not particularly helpful. More fruitful is, "What is it we are ambitious for?" If we see "ambitious" as equivalent to "driven" or "goal-oriented," we need to ask what it is we are driven toward; what is our overarching goal?

> Humility is a proper estimation of oneself: a healthy, God-shaped understanding of both our gifts and potential for His service, as well as the limitations we bring.

There are two wrong ways to deal with the issue of ambition. The first is to pursue our agenda rather than God's. The second is not to pursue our agenda out of a false humility. Like many issues surrounding guidance, the question of "appropriate ambition" doesn't lend itself to simple, clear-cut answers. But if we avoid the excesses of these two extremes, we'll find ourselves on middle ground that is far more likely to be the place where God would have us stand.

Pursuing Our Agenda Rather than God's

Typically, our culture honors those who have a successful career, material goods, celebrity status, power, or have attained similar goals. All around us, and from our earliest days, we're pressured into being "successful" and to strive after goals like these. But, by themselves, these are all what J. Oswald Sanders calls "unworthy ambitions." It's helpful to distinguish, as he does, between worthy and unworthy ambitions, and it's on the latter we need to concentrate here. Unworthy goals are any that are outside God's desires for our lives. If we're committed to a successful career in teaching in the community where we grew up, that may be exactly what God wants of us. Our ambition to make the best contribution in this setting is good and well, and pleasing to God. On the other hand, if God has repeatedly been calling us to seminary and full-time youth work, and we ignore or stifle that call, even if we attain great success teaching, we haven't gladdened God's heart. If this example has a familiar sound, it should. Jesus said, "What good will it be for a man if he gains the whole world, yet forfeits his soul? Or what can a man give in exchange for his soul?" (Matthew 16:26).

If we fear that we're seeking our goals rather than God's, it's time to check our motives and priorities. What exactly is most important in our lives? What is your honest answer to this question: Are you genuinely open to seeking God's leading in your life, wherever it may lead, or are you already committed to a path that will further your success? These could be the same thing, but if you have any doubts about your motives, it's crucial to be honest with yourself.

At the root of any discussion on ambition lies the issue of our motives and our sense of direction. In other words, what we're talking about here is our definition of "success," and how God understands that concept.

By our society's standards, a life lived in quiet service of others, on lifelong subsistence wages, with no public recognition, is far from a success. Yet that life, if lived in a quiet obedience to and reliance on God, may fit exactly His definition of "successful" Christian living. Former U.S. Senator Mark Hatfield comments, "There is no success for the Christian other than being faithful to God's will and call."

Scripture makes it clear, in one example after another, how God calls people to positions of leadership and authority. The Old and New Testament heroes of the faith are presented as people who showed godly ambition, taking on the responsibility that God brought their way. While their contemporaries may have seen them as successful, far more important is that their obedience and readiness to further

God's kingdom made them successes in *His* eyes. At times, Scripture is also explicit in telling us that seeking after leadership roles and responsibility are worthy goals. Paul tells Timothy, for example, "Here is a saying you may trust: 'To aspire to leadership is an honorable ambition'" (1 Timothy 3:1, REV).

J. Oswald Sanders on Ambition . . .

God wants men who . . . are discontented with a limited opportunity when they could bring greater glory to God in a wider sphere. Our ambition should be for a wider influence for God, a deeper love toward God, a stronger faith in God, and a growing knowledge of God.

To counter wrong-headed motives and a misunderstanding of success, we might speak of a "holy ambition," one pleasing to God and honoring Him. Is our ambition aimed at advancing God's kingdom or our own interests? Is our ambition aimed at furthering God's reputation or our own? If we suspect we're putting ourselves first, then we're quite probably right—and need to adjust our thinking accordingly.

God's Understanding of Success

Success is living in such a way that you are using what God has given you—your intellect, abilities and energy—to reach the purpose he intends for your life.

—Kathi Hudson[1]

Not Pursuing Our Agenda Out of False Humility

The second danger is to lapse into a false piety. That's when we fool ourselves into thinking that any success is sinful, and that we should shun anything that smacks of success. We rightly seek to minimize pride and selfish ambitions, but wrongly assume worthy ends cannot have good motives.

For example, is any ego involved when a pastor accepts a call that moves him or her from a 500-member church to one three times that size? Or when we accept a promotion that will bring us considerable prestige and a generous increase? Only the most saintly of us could avoid all sense of pride in those situations. If we waited until we were so sanctified that we'd be able to make all decisions without any hint of selfish interest, we'd decide almost nothing. God neither expects nor demands that we operate at that high level of sanctified thinking. But just because we can't be sure we're making a totally "untainted" decision, one free of all selfish interest, that doesn't mean we should do nothing. On the contrary, the lessons from Scripture are that God takes sinful and sometimes reluctant people, and when we're willing to be used by Him, He enables us to accomplish great things for His kingdom.

> If we waited until we were so sanctified that we'd be able to make all decisions without any hint of selfish interest, we'd decide almost nothing.

We need to bring to our thinking on guidance a modesty, a genuine humility, and a sense of awe that God uses sinful people like us for His purposes. That's having a proper estimate of ourselves. But that's not the end of the story. God enlists us in His service, and with His commitment to equip us to do His will, we tread on dangerous turf when we say, as Peter did in response to his vision, "No, Lord!" (Acts 10:14, REV). For one thing, saying "No" and "Lord" in the same breath are a contradiction in terms for any Christian. Then, as we see in the next verse, we—like Peter—are told that "It is not for you to call profane what God counts clean" (Acts 10:15, REV). When God is calling us to do things that we think may make us look inappropriately self-serving or successful—in other words, something we think looks "profane"—it is we who need to make adjustments, not God.

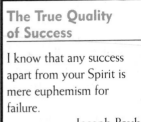

The True Quality of Success

I know that any success apart from your Spirit is mere euphemism for failure.

—Joseph Bayly

How *can* we know if it's our motives and unworthy ambition that are calling us in a certain direction, or God's leading? As we honestly address this question, through **Prayer [3]** and a careful look at the inevitable nature of our **Mixed Motives [54]**, we may come away still unsure that we are taking the right step for the right reason. That's the time to avoid getting into some spiral of indecision, and instead transcend the **Doubts [48]** that can beset our thinking. After we've gone through the various steps outlined elsewhere in this book, we will be placed to move ahead—sidetracked neither by our selfish ambitions nor by an equally damaging false piety.

Think About It

- What would happen if there were no ambitious Christians? Can God's work get done without amibitous Christians?
- What's the difference between true humility, which rightly accepts responsibility, and false humility, which rejects it?
- How much of Jesus' temptation in the wilderness had to do with ambition? How did He face these temptations? What lessons can I learn from Jesus' life and ministry about the nature of ambition and the temptations it brings?
- It's said of Moses that he spent forty years thinking he was somebody, forty years learning he was a nobody, and forty years learning what God could do with a nobody. How did his "ambitions" change during those three periods, and which of those three most closely parallels my life right now?
- In Micah 6:8 we're told, "To act justly and to love mercy and to walk humbly with your God." How do we attain this humility the prophet refers to that would steer us between the errors listed above?

44 Calling

Don't confuse a "need" with a "call"—needs are plentiful, calls are few, and calls that God makes of you are few indeed.

Thinking you may be called to full-time ministry? Or to mission work? Or to move from your present job in Alabama to one in Wyoming? How do you know if God's voice is calling you, or if you're simply talking to yourself in response to your own desires and wishes? What, after all, is a call, and how do you know if what you're hearing is a call?

We tend to think of a call as God's clear intervention in our lives, in which He asks us to serve Him in some capacity. Typically we're talking about full-time work, quite possibly in what we've traditionally seen as areas of ministry—but not necessarily so.

It's easy for Christians to succumb to hearing calls that aren't there, for several reasons. One is that we see a need and incorrectly conclude that God wants us to help meet that need. (See **The Need Versus the Call [46].**) Another reason that flows from a misguided super-spirituality is that some Christians think those who are involved in full-time ministry (especially sacrificial ministry) are more spiritual and somehow "better" believers. A third reason is that some assume that only work resulting from a clear sense of call is legitimate Christian work. It may be, for example, that you're a schoolteacher or a computer technician, but that you've never felt an actual call to your position. Maybe you feel that you just "ended up" where you have, and think that because God has never called you to what you're doing, you should keep waiting for Him to steer you to your "real" job or ministry.

You may identify other reasons, but the fact is there's much fuzzy and potentially dangerous thinking associated with the idea of "God calling us" to a ministry, task, or commitment. One major danger is thinking that we even need some kind of special calling to do God's work. J. Oswald Sanders points out that Scripture gives us ample guidance on the work to which He calls His people. Writing in the context of mission work, he says that we need no call other than certain Scriptures "to lead us to recognize the general obligation resting on all believers. If we see a man drowning, and we ourselves can swim, we do not need a special direction to make us go to his rescue." While we should recognize that Christians are all called to tasks such as evangelism, support of missions, stewardship, and so on, we tend to think of a call in more particular terms.

Below are ten sets of questions to help you think through the possibility that God is talking to you in a more particular way, and that you need to listen. On the other hand, you may be in no danger of hearing a call that isn't there; you may have heard a call clearly enough but are stalling in responding to God. Whatever your position, the questions below should be a helpful start. Answering these questions will help you determine if this call is the real thing. Of course, you'll want to apply other thinking, like working through **The Big Five [1],** before answering.

1. *Can I put in writing (a sentence, a paragraph, or even a few pages) exactly why I think God is calling me?* If not, what does that tell me? Also, am I clear that I have heard a call? Remember, a "call" is something you *hear*, not something you *feel*. If today you *feel* called to a certain task or ministry, by next week your feelings may have changed. If you've *heard* a call, it will be valid today, next Wednesday, and in the years ahead.

2. *Is there a specific need that God has brought to my attention, to which I'm feeling drawn (working with inner-city youth in Chicago)?* Or is this a more general sense of calling (into full-time pastoral ministry)? While I know either is legitimate, am I clear on the difference? If not, what does that tell me?

3. *To what extent am I clear that this is God calling me?* In other words, how confident am I that it's *God's* script I'm following, and that I'm not simply standing offstage calling out lines that I would *like* Him to include in the part He has for me? How much is this call at God's initiative, and how much have I been offering Him helpful hints or suggestions on what He might like to tell me?

Frederick Buechner on Calling . . .

By and large a good rule for finding out [your calling] is this. The kind of work God usually calls you to is the kind of work (a) that you need most to do and (b) that the world most needs to have done. . . . The place God calls you to is the place where your deep gladness and the world's deep hunger meet.

If I'm honest, how much are my motives shaped by reasons honoring God, and how much by my own agenda?

4. *Have I considered carefully what motivations might underlie my sense of call?* This is important because I realize it's so easy to deceive myself into thinking I'm hearing a call when I'm not. If I'm honest, how much are my motives shaped by reasons honoring God, and how much by my own agenda (for example, my ambition or a desire to please my parents)? Derek Tidball, in his book *How Does God Guide?*, has listed several possible factors that can easily lead us into acting incorrectly upon what we think is God's call. Among these are escapism (see number six below for more on this), a romantic or idealized notion of full-time Christian service, dishonest motives (such as seeking power or esteem), and guilt over not responding to a need.[2]

5. *What do mature Christians in my life think of my sense of call?* Do they think it makes sense? Does my wife/husband/fiancé/pastor think it makes sense? Many Christians agree that a call should be confirmed by others. Is that the case in my situation? If not, what does that tell me?

6. *Is this sense of calling prompted by unhappiness or discontent in my present situation?* If so, how can I be sure I am not simply being tempted to seek greener pastures, and trying to put a spiritual veneer on running away from a tough situation? God may well be calling me from a place of unhappiness to somewhere else, but am I being honest about how much there's a push from one place and a God-directed pull to another? Am I in danger of doing what seems like the right thing for a wrong reason? It doesn't matter how spiritual, self-sacrificial, or noble the cause, if you're pursuing it for the wrong reason, you're asking for trouble.

> **Send Me!**
>
> Then I heard the voice of the Lord saying, "Whom shall I send? And who will go for us?"
> And I said, "Here am I. Send me!"
>
> —Isaiah 6:8

Startled at the Call

When you want position, beware of position. But when you are called because you are worthy, when you are startled at the call, you can afford to take the place in life that beckons and bids you come.
— Martin Grove Brumbaugh

7. *Do my gifts, likes, dislikes, personality, skills, and training fit me for the call?* Or, more significantly, are there any weaknesses that present significant barriers to my fulfilling this call? Yes, God can overcome or compensate for any weaknesses we may have. Most of the time, however, He seems to call people to tasks for which they're already gifted and have some inclination. We ought to respond to any call with great humility, in awe that God wants to use us for *any* task in His kingdom. We don't sense a call to every need we encounter, but when we do, and when there's a major gap between our capacity and the task that beckons, we need to think through this discrepancy with godly friends. (See **Equipping the Called [45].**)

8. *How compelling is my sense of call?* Is this a longstanding, increasingly growing conviction that God wants me to move in a certain direction? Or is it a sudden, recent development? And, if I'm honest, am I a member of the "call of the month club," falling in love with whatever is the most recent need I heard about? Many in the ministry have said something like this: "You should enter the ministry only if you can't stay out." Is my sense of calling equally compelling? Or do I see it simply as one of several options I might pursue?

9. *What are the costs of misreading a "call"?* If I'm unsure that this call is authentic, what are the costs of acting now and learning later that this wasn't in fact God's calling? What harm is there in waiting to see if God provides greater clarity later? If God wants to get word to me, He'll find a way. Is there any compelling need for me to act upon this now? If I'm unsure, what are the costs of waiting and seeking greater clarity from God?

10. *Am I acting upon what I already know?* If I'm at the other end of the spectrum, and am sure I have heard God's call but haven't yet responded, the question is simple: "Why not?" Henry Parry Liddon wrote, "Nothing is really lost by a life of sacrifice; everything is lost by failure to obey God's call." Enough said.

See also **Testing, Testing [16]; Waiting [40]; Ambition [43]; Equipping the Called [45]; The Need Versus the Call [46].**

45 Equipping the Called

In whatever arena of life you live out a calling, you should remember that God calls some He has already equipped and will equip all others whom He has called.

Two possible barriers to guidance are our reluctance to hear when God calls us to something for which we think we're ill-equipped, and when He's *not* calling us in an area where we think we're pretty darn good. It's the first issue we want to focus on here. (For some thoughts on the second, see **Hubris [51].**)

Our sense of inadequacy for God's call may come either from who we are ("Lord, I just don't think I have the skills for Bible translation work") or the context to which we are called ("Lord, I know I have gifts as a teacher, but how can I apply these in a Muslim country?").

The answers God gave Moses are helpful. At a human level, Moses brought a mixed bag of skills to the task of leading the children of Israel out of Egypt. He'd been educated in Pharaoh's court and knew how the political system worked at the highest levels. Yet he was an outsider—and had been for a long time—both to the Egyptian power system and to the children of Israel. How could either group be expected to take him seriously? His excuses and protests that he wasn't right for the job seem perfectly reasonable—until you consider who has called him.

God then shows Moses in one dramatic way after another who is doing the calling, dealing with Moses' reluctance to take on this task. He accepts this call, grudgingly, but as he depends on God one step at a time, he and the children of Israel are indeed delivered from the Egyptians and brought to the edge of the Promised Land because of Moses' obedience.

It's through this obedience that Moses, and we, learn an important lesson about calling and being equipped. By relying on God to help us take the first step we learn we can fully trust His leading. That lesson includes knowing that it is only in God's power that we can accomplish His purposes. We might not see in our lives the

In the Right Place

The will of God will never lead you where the grace of God cannot keep you.

—Unknown

> ## God's Supply
>
> Cast yourself into the arms of God and be very sure that if he wants anything of you, he will fit you for the work and give you strength.
> —Philip Neri

sequence of astonishing miracles that God did through Moses. But, like him, we learn through obedience that we increasingly need to depend on God and His power to enable us to accomplish the specific work to which He has called us and His general call to us to live holy lives that are pleasing to Him.

Like Moses, the more closely we walk with God as we try to honor His specific and general calls in our lives, the better we will get to know Him—and be aware of our need to rely on Him. It's no coincidence that at one of the high points of Moses' journey with God, when He reveals His glory to Moses, this great leader asks a profoundly important question: "Then Moses said to [the Lord], 'If your Presence does not go with us, do not send us up from here. How will anyone know that you are pleased with me and with your people unless you go with us?'" (Exodus 33:15-16). Let us too never move forward from where we now stand unless God's presence goes with us. But let us also not hold back when He calls. Throughout Scripture, we see people like Moses whom God equipped for His work. Our part in God's work, of proclaiming and living out the gospel message, continues today—and so does His equipping us to do it.

See also **Excuses, Excuses [32]; The Need Versus the Call [46]; Calling [44]; Courage [47].**

46 The Need Versus the Call

It's important to distinguish between the needs in the world God undoubtedly wants addressed, and those to which He's calling you.

Last Sunday you thought you unmistakably sensed God's call when you attended a mission presentation about service opportunities in Central America. The speaker so effectively painted a picture of urgent need that you almost caught your breath wondering, "Is this what You're wanting of me, Lord?" In Monday's mail came an appeal from a Christian organization, which you've long supported, that stressed its need for full-time workers among the rural poor in another area. Again, you found yourself strangely compelled to ask again, "Is *this* what You're wanting of me, Lord?" Then, on Tuesday you heard about that fledgling Christian college in Eastern Europe . . . well, you get the picture.

We're barraged daily by the claims of a world riddled with valid needs: to spread the gospel message, for Bible translation, for spiritual growth, for development relief, for crisis help, and to fill a seemingly unending range of opportunities for service. Each of these needs represents some gap or hurt in people's lives that God would dearly like to see addressed. Might God be tapping you on the shoulder, saying, "Take a look over here—I've got something to show you"? You need God to answer this question: How do I differentiate between these needs and what may be Your call?

The first suggestion is to free ourselves from any strange notions that we somehow must respond to multiple needs. While our heads tell us we can do only one of the things to which we may feel called, our hearts have higher aspirations. We see so much need and hurt that we want to do more. God will call us only to one part of His kingdom—or, at least, to only one part at a time.

We also shouldn't think that only full-time Christian service constitutes a "real" calling. There's no biblical mandate whatever for seeing work as an accountant, computer analyst, librarian, or electrician as a "lesser" calling than pastoral work or mission service. Regardless of the place God calls us, we're all engaged in holy service in whatever work we're doing. Finding that place often is not easy, although the section on **Calling [44]** has some pointers. Even more important than what God is calling you to *do*, however, is what He is calling you to *be*.

In distinguishing between God's general and specific call to Christians, John Stott notes that God first calls us to be a certain kind of person. We are to be disciples of Jesus Christ. In that sense, he says, "We all share in the same general call of God; we have each received a different particular call from God." As we seek to discover that particular call, we can do so confident that He will direct us through what may be a maze of possible opportunities. Needs may abound, but without being insensitive to any of them, we must move forward to seek that one place in God's kingdom where He would have us serve.

See also **Equipping the Called [45].**

faithful

If I am faithful to the duties of

the present, God will provide for the future.

Gregory T. Bedell

to the

Present

Be strong and courageous.
Do not be terrified;
do not be discouraged,
for the LORD your God
will be with you
wherever you go.

Joshua 1:9

Overcoming Concerns

47 Courage

Expect decision making to be a difficult, sometimes anguished process that may demand courageous action, but we're assured by God Himself that He will empower and sustain us at every step.

A central theme of this book is that God *will* lead you in the choices you need to make. But nowhere does the Bible suggest that discerning His will is an easy task, or that living out our choices is easy sailing either. Either or both of those steps can be extremely difficult, requiring great integrity and courage on our part, as well as a great measure of grace from God. Making important decisions is hard work.

The difficulty lies in the implications of what may come next, beyond the decision itself: *acting out* your choice. It may mean you've made the tough decision to quit a job on principle, knowing you have no immediate likelihood of finding another position. While reaching the decision may have been an anguished task, now you need to take a stand—and live with the pain, fear, or other consequences that will come your way.

Jesus said that a life of discipleship, and the choices it at times involves, would prove to be costly. He spoke, for example, of the costs of discipleship when He told anyone who would come after Him to "take up his cross and follow me" (Matthew 16:24). How might these costs be manifested? It may be how family or friends respond to a particular decision we've made. They may simply fail to support us, or, worse still, actively oppose or resist our position. Pressures may come from work, from society in general, even from fellow Christians. Or we ourselves may be our most effective foes, as we second-guess our decisions, waver on implementing them, or pull back and change our minds after taking a clear stand.

While we can't know in advance where difficulties may arise, we can be sure that we'll often need courage to act. Dietrich Bonhoeffer put it quite bluntly: "When Christ calls a man he bids him come and die." That statement applies not only to our initial commitment, but also to a willingness to daily present our lives as "living sacrifices" (Romans 12:1), always willing to do whatever task God puts before us. Nothing provides a better example of courage and obedience to God's will than Jesus' coming through the agony of Gethsemane still willing to go to the cross.

We can't predict what levels of courage we might need to make the hard choices that lie ahead, or the equally hard commitments to live out those choices. We do know, however, that God will give us the grace and power we need to live out His will. And lest for a moment we think God is somehow indebted to us because of any courageous, costly choices we make, let us recall the words of Meister Eckhart: "How can we ever be the sold short or the cheated, we who for every service have long ago been overpaid."

See also **Obedience [57].**

48 Doubts

Expect and welcome doubts in guidance. But once you've made a decision, get beyond your doubts.

Ten Thoughts for Dealing with Doubt

1. What exactly is it about guidance that you're doubting? Is it the *willingness* of God to show you His will? *His ability* to show you His will? *Your ability* to understand or recognize His will when you see it? Your *confidence* that it was in fact God's will that you thought you saw? Your *worthiness* to receive God's will? Or something else? (Checking the "Guidance Road Map" on pages 13 and 14 might be helpful.)

2. Know that doubts are normal and you're normal for having them. Some of the greatest figures in the history of the church have been plagued by doubt in their faith journeys, such as Saint Ignatius of Loyola, Søren Kierkegaard, and Martin Luther. These saints of earlier days were okay, and having doubts is okay for you too.

3. If you're going to have doubts, let them serve you—don't you serve *them.* In other words, use doubts to prod you to ask hard questions, to scrutinize the implications of the options you're considering, to hold your decision up to the light of Scripture. When you've worked through the issues, though, make your decision and move on. Treat doubt like a confusing intersection on the highway that forced you to pull off the road and consult the map; now that you've confirmed you're headed the right way, why do you want to return to the point where you were perplexed?

4. "Never doubt in the dark what God told you in the light," said V. Raymond Edman. He was right.

5. God doesn't get angry with us because we doubt. Consider Jesus' love for Thomas, the one who would believe only when he saw the nail marks and put his hand into Jesus' side. Jesus appeared before him—without anger—to address him and his doubts head-on, telling the disciple, "Stop doubting and believe" (John 20:27).

6. As He did with Thomas, Jesus will meet us and our doubts head-on, but on His terms and in His time.

> **Answer the Door!**
>
> Doubt comes in at the window when inquiry is denied at the door.
> —Benjamin Jowett

7. If you doubt because you think your faith is deficient, consider two things. First, who of us has *enough* faith to please God? Second, it is God Himself who gives us the gift of faith, and if we lack faith He will "help . . . [our] unbelief" (Mark 9:24). (See **Conditional Guidance [21].**) Even if our faith is as simple as that of the woman who touched the hem of His robe, it will suffice. Even if our faith is like that of Peter sinking into the water when his faith failed him, but who still kept his eyes on Christ, it will suffice. Let's bring to God what limited faith we have, and let Him grow and multiply it.

8. Be especially wary of the kind of doubt mentioned in James 1:6-8, in which James cautions that when we ask anything of God, we "must believe and not doubt, because he who doubts is like a wave of the sea, blown and tossed by the wind. . . . [H]e is a double-minded man, unstable in all he does." Here James is referring not to the normal misgivings and fears that assail people of faith as much as he's warning against a faith that has split loyalties—to God and to something else. The Greek word for "double-minded" literally refers to someone who is "double-souled." While God welcomes our honest doubts, He feels quite differently about divided loyalties. Andrew McNab comments on this passage: "Doubt, hesitancy about God, dependence on something or someone other than God are in reality unbelief."[1]

9. Don't confuse doubts with difficulties that arise after you've made a careful decision. If necessary, think back to when you made your decision and review the reasons you decided the way you did. If you decided carefully back then, why are you doubting your choice now? Just because you're facing tough going, it doesn't mean you're on the wrong road. (See **Pulling Up in Unbelief [58]; When Guidance "Goes Wrong" [59].**)

10. Always keep your eyes on Christ and the cross. "Every step toward Christ kills a doubt," said Theodore Ledyard Cuyler. "Every thought, word, and deed for him carries you away from discouragement." See also **Testing, Testing [16]; Courage [47].**

The Cost of Timidity

Half the failures of this world arise from pulling in one's horse as he is leaping.

—Julius Hare and Augustus Hare

49 Five Groundless Fears

Beware of groundless fears that can keep you from finding and living out God's will.

Figuring out God's will is complex enough as it is. So it's a real mystery why we make things even harder by bringing a grocery sack full of unwarranted fears to the process. This isn't the place to explore the reasons we do that. What does need attention, though, are five fears that can deafen us or distract us as we try to hear God's voice.

Five Fears That Distract Us from Hearing God's Voice

1. I'm afraid God won't speak to me.
2. Even if He does speak, I'm afraid I won't hear or understand Him.
3. My personal history of failure or sin makes it unlikely that God will have anything to say to me.
4. If I do His will, I might fail—then where would I be?
5. I'm afraid God might lead me where I don't want to go.

Let's look at these groundless fears one by one. The fact that you're reading this book probably means you don't genuinely believe number one—at least, not on the surface. You already *assume and expect* that God will guide you. But even if you have doubts about that, the promises noted in **Key Scripture Verses [60]** should set you straight in a hurry. Take a look, too, at **The "Abba, Father" Principle [18]**. Scripture repeatedly refers to God as a loving, tender parent who both wants the best for us and promises to show us His ways if we genuinely seek after Him. If you're serious about your faith, you have God's word that not only will He guide

His people, He will guide you individually. In brief, the idea that God won't speak to me is utterly without foundation.

Number two may sound more credible: "After all, who am I, a mere sinful mortal, to presume I will be in tune with any messages that God may send my way?" But on closer inspection, this fear also evaporates. Again, the problem is misunderstanding how God deals with us. Surely we're in danger of insulting Him and His love for us if we think He has neither the motivation nor the means to get through to us. Assuming as always that we're serious about seeking His will (reread **Conditional Guidance [21]** if necessary), we can rest assured He won't hide it from us. M. Blaine Smith says Jesus promises "a shepherd's guidance, which means he'll take the full responsibility to see that we get where he wants us to go when we are open to his leading. . . . He's simply too big to allow our lack of understanding to keep him from leading us in the path of his will."

> Just as God has the answers to our sinfulness, He is also a specialist in fixing the broken and transforming failure into success in His kingdom.

Fear number three concerning our own history of failure or sin once again reflects an inadequate grasp of what God promises those who commit their lives to Him. There's nothing, repeat nothing, that we've done that is too big of a problem for God to deal with. Philip Yancey writes in *What's So Amazing About Grace?* that "There is nothing we can do to make God love us more. There is nothing we can do to make God love us less." It's normal enough to fear failure that results from bad choices we may make. It's also reasonable to fear failure that may result from our well-intended choices, the ones we thought God was leading us toward. (See **When Guidance "Goes Wrong" [59]**.) How we define "failure," however, is important. God's definition of failure and ours don't always overlap. The world around us may define as failure what God sees as faithful and obedient service, and we may be all too ready to accept the world's message that we failed, rather than God's. Being unfaithful or disobedient to God's call or expectations should get our attention, not what we see as failure. Just as God has the answers to our sinfulness, He is also a specialist in fixing the broken and transforming failure into success in His kingdom.

Assuming, though, that we actually have disappointed God and not just ourselves, we need to be reminded of two realities: that "all have sinned and fall short of the glory of God, and are justified freely by his grace through the redemption that came by Christ Jesus" (Romans 3:23-24). We are joined by the entire human race in the extent to which we have failed God. We also join those millions throughout history who make up the church universal when we accept God's grace and His justification in our lives.

Number four, a fear of failure, also seems reasonable enough. We will fail at times. But the real issue isn't failure itself; it's how we—and God—deal with that failure.

It may be helpful to look carefully at how we define failure. Remember the old saying that God doesn't call us to be successful; He calls us to be faithful. In looking at any potential failures that may lie ahead, it helps to know how God sees them. Maybe fourteen years in a seemingly bleak and fruitless mission enterprise is a complete failure by human standards. But if that time was lived out in faithful obedience to God, He is still working out His purposes that fit perfectly with His definition of success.

What if the failure is plain enough, arising clearly from our mistakes or even sinful conduct? Again, it's time to remember that God works only with people who have in some way "failed"—and He is capable of redeeming and working out for His purposes anything that we've done.

Finally, there's number five, the fear that you don't know where God's guidance may take you—and it may be to places you don't want to go. Let's face it, guidance often leads to uncomfortable results. The section on **Change [8]** makes clear that we won't always welcome what God has in store for us. And as **Doors—Open and Closed [10]** indicates, going where God wants comes with no guarantees that the path will be easy. This is the most justifiable of the fears, for it's well based in reality. Instead

Love Knows No Fear

There is no fear in love.
But perfect love drives out
fear. . . . The one who fears
is not made perfect in love.
— 1 John 4:18

of asking if guidance may take us places we don't want to go (sometimes it undoubtedly will), the question we should instead ask is, "Why exactly do we fear where He may lead?" Forcing ourselves to answer that question may yield some uncomfortable results. Are we in effect saying we don't think God knows what He's doing? Or are we saying God is something of a killjoy who wants us to live grim, puritanical lives? (See **The Scrooge Pitfall [55].**) Or do we fear that His calling will be too hard for us to honor? Whatever our answers, we're likely to realize that we have greatly underestimated God and His astonishing love for us. He who knows us better than we know ourselves, and watches over us with a love beyond measure, seeks only our best. Forcing ourselves to look closely at this and our other fears concerning guidance will make us face anew whatever weaknesses mark our relationship with God. And that's a healthy move, whether we're in "guidance-seeking" mode or not.

50 Guilt

Guilt is a negative, obstructionist force in seeking God's will, and can easily seduce us from the paths we should follow.

Guilt and guidance are a lousy mix. Guilt is a negative, corrosive force. Like **Worry [56]**, if it's not dealt with, guilt does nothing productive and only gets in the way of us living the lives and making the choices God would have us pursue. Guilt can warp our thinking on guidance if we lose sight of certain basics. For example, maybe you're planning to say "no" to someone who's asked you to marry him, but you feel terribly guilty about the prospect of hurting him. Or perhaps you'd promised to teach junior high Sunday school this year but are now thinking of breaking that commitment. In the first case, you're entitled to feel bad about hurting someone, but if you're doing the right thing (and know that sweet and caring though he is, he's not the guy for you), then guilt is hardly the issue. In the second case, guilt may well be in order.

The point? Like worry, guilt is useful only if it spurs us on to fixing what needs attention. If we're making the right decisions, we have no need to feel guilt. Discomfort, perhaps, but not guilt. If we're afraid we may make a decision about which we may feel guilty, surely that's warning enough to rethink that decision.

51 Hubris—Christian Style

Beware of assuming too easily that we can do anything we think God has called us to do; not only can we do nothing on our own, we need to be certain we've heard correctly in the first place.

What in the World Is "Hubris"?

Hubris is a term from classical Greek literature meaning pride or arrogance that leads to a tragic downfall. In responding to God's guidance, Christians can display a kind of pride that, if not checked, can lead to unhappy outcomes. That pride is spawned and nurtured by a culture that tells us we can accomplish virtually whatever we set out to do. Yet that philosophy will quickly lead us to have misplaced confidence in the role we actually play in God's service.

Charles Spurgeon defined humility as "having a proper estimation of ourselves." As we look at the decisions and actions in which God guides us, we must always remember that it is *God* who guides us, for *His* purposes, for tasks to be accomplished in *His* strength. The moment we begin moving to the point where we think of these tasks as *our* work into which we have invited God's participation, we begin to get into trouble.

Paul wrote, "I can do everything through him who gives me strength" (Philippians 4:13). The implication is clearly that he's talking about everything that's in keeping with God's will, not anything that Paul happens to have in mind.

Therefore, all power is ours as we go about God's work. We must remember, though, that both the power and the work are God's. Drifting from that perspective constitutes the beginning of Christian hubris; we need to halt that move before it leads we know not where.

52 Indecision (or The Paralysis of Analysis)

Remember that the difference between thorough, thoughtful processing of **The Big Five [1]** *and sustained dithering and indecisiveness is that the latter brings no honor to God.*

Making decisions is hard work; making godly decisions is holy work. But making decisions also requires completed work, and if you find yourself taking longer than you know is appropriate to come to a conclusion, it's helpful to ask why. You may be delaying on a decision for good reasons. (See **Waiting [40].**) If you know yourself well enough to realize that you normally struggle on deciding anything important, it's time to look closely at that pattern.

Making decisions is hard work; making godly decisions is holy work.

Precisely why are you inclined to dither and delay? One possibility is that you always want more information to shape your decision. Of course, getting the data you need is crucial. But you may have reached the point where you're not gathering any additional useful data. You're quite possibly obsessing with seeking completeness or perfection in finding out what you need to know when that simply isn't possible. As Samuel Butler said, "Life is the art of drawing sufficient conclusions from insufficient premises."

Alternatively, you might simply be procrastinating, trying to avoid dealing with the unpleasant reality you know you face—having to make a decision. When you've carefully worked your way through **The Big Five [1],** you should be close to a decision-making point. If you're not, ask yourself why you're unable or unwilling to decide. Is it plain old indecisiveness? Or is it fear of the consequences of your decision? Is it perhaps a lack of trust in what God might have in store? You could well be dealing with one or more of the **Five Groundless Fears [49].**

Maybe you have a good reason for delaying the decision. If you're prone to being indecisive, you already know you're that kind of person. You probably also know what you need to do: set a deadline, promise God that with His help you'll make the best decision you can by that time, and then do so.

See also **Godly Decision Making [36].**

53 The Law of Unintended Consequences

Taking ill-advised action can set in motion a spiritual chain reaction that you may greatly regret.

A couple of points on this.

First, don't rely on others to determine God's will for you. For example, don't propose marriage to someone you're highly undecided about, thinking that if she (or he) says "yes," then it must be God's will for you both. That approach is a total abdication of your responsibility to thoughtfully and prayerfully reach a clear decision.

The philosophy that says we should live boldly, taking chances as we live our lives to the fullest, is fine—so long as the chances fit in the "adventurous" rather than "reckless" category. There's a marked difference between living boldly by trying the "Squirrel Soufflé" at that exotic new restaurant in town, and cavalierly proposing marriage to someone. If you're fortunate enough to have proposed to someone who has a healthier commitment to spiritual discernment than you do, maybe your own thoughtlessness will be effectively counterbalanced. But what if the object of your halfhearted affections is as ill formed in her (or his) thinking as you are? What if you are *both* being superficial, or even irresponsible, in seeking God's mind on this matter? Quite simply, the issue is to accept full responsibility for your own decisions and choices, and not hand over what amounts to a proxy vote to someone else.

As the section on **Choices, Choices [20]** notes, some decisions are minor enough not to deserve much attention. Deciding which fast food restaurant to visit is not something that merits hours of prayer and thought; you and your friends could well choose between McDonald's and Burger King by **Flipping a Coin [34].** But to take that approach to a major decision, such as you and your spouse deciding whether to adopt a child, is ridiculous. In brief, not taking seriously our obligations to seek God's guidance on important issues can trigger much trouble.

Take Traffic Violations, for Example

Generally, traffic violations fit into two categories—negligence and recklessness. The first are the sins of omission, the acts of neglect where we're not paying enough attention. The second are the sins of commission, those acts of deliberate foolishness and disregard for our well-being and the safety of others. The Law of Unintended Consequences can be triggered by either kind of action. Neglecting to seek out God's will on an important issue, whether through thoughtlessness, impulsiveness, or any other cause, can cause problems. Perhaps the problems will be all the greater if we, in what is really an act of spiritual recklessness, deliberately refuse to do what we know God expects of us: check in with Him. Either way, the consequences are the same. Even if we've chosen the right path, the way we got there is surely displeasing to Him.

Second, if we've taken a step that has set in motion a ripple of other implications because we didn't seek God's leading, the good news is that He is Lord over those unintended consequences as well. As the section titled **When Guidance "Goes Wrong" [59]** makes clear, God can redeem even our errors—including those of neglect, recklessness, omission, and commission. To be sure, Scripture assures us that God is always ready to welcome back our repentant hearts. And yes, there may be some consequences for which we'll still be accountable. The main question is, though, why not try avoiding the fallout that inevitably follows from this spiritual law in the first place?

54 Mixed Motives

Even though our sinful natures make it impossible to act from pure motives, being aware of this as we seek God's leading will itself reduce the contamination.

If you've just read one of those frightening magazine articles that tells you how many bacteria and impurities are in our food, you might be tempted to stop eating altogether. Those occasional reminders of things like e-coli and other hazards are important, as they prevent us from taking needless risks in preparing and eating food. But obviously, we need to keep on eating. Sobered though we may be, we know that giving up food simply isn't an option.

With guidance, too, we know we work in a contaminated environment. All our motives, thinking, and decision making are contaminated to some extent by our sinful natures. That's a reality we should always remember. While we need to take sensible precautions, we should never become obsessive about sin's capacity to undermine the quality of our guidance. The very act of going through the guidance process, in confident dependence that God will lead us, will counteract our sinful tendencies.

The contamination of our motives is real enough; after all, we are fallen creatures. In Romans 3:23, Paul told us that "all have sinned and fallen short of the glory of God." And in Jeremiah 17:9 we read, "The heart is deceitful above all things and beyond cure." Those of us who have committed our lives to serving Christ don't need to be reminded of our capacity for sinful conduct. If our thinking stops at that point, however, then we might as well quit our quest for guidance. If we're so inclined to our wicked ways, how can we possibly hope to hear God's voice clearly, let alone have the capacity to obey it?

Fortunately, as we know, the story doesn't end there. The next step in our Christian walk

> ## Food for the Journey
>
> Then Jesus declared, "I am the bread of life. He who comes to me will never go hungry, and he who believes in me will never be thirsty."
>
> —John 6:35

Know My Heart, My Thoughts

Search me, O God, and know my heart; test me and know my anxious thoughts. See if there is any offensive way in me, and lead me in the way everlasting.

—Psalm 139:23-24

is sanctification, that process by which we increasingly become like Jesus Himself. This astonishing reality means that we acquire the ability to think more like God, and increasingly to align our wills with His. (For more on this idea, see **Clear Thinking [9].**)

This capacity allows us to make decisions that are pleasing to God. But not all our thoughts and decisions fit in that category. For the rest of our lives, we'll continue to make sinful decisions and fail at times to recognize how God is leading us. Therefore, we're left with a dilemma. No matter how earnestly we seek God's will on certain matters, at some level our thinking will be contaminated by our own selfish wills. How do we cope with this reality?

God knows that we approach decisions with mixed motives. If we're serious about seeking His will, He'll cut through whatever barriers may exist—including our sinful natures—to tell us what we need to know.

Gloria Gaither, in *Decisions: A Christian's Approach to Making Right Choices*, suggests several questions to help neutralize the selfishness we inevitably bring to this process:

- What is my number one motive? Am I really seeking "the path of everlasting life"?
- Am I thinking honestly in regard to material goals?
- Am I responding to peer pressure or public opinion?
- Would I choose "right" even if it appears to be occupational, financial, or social suicide?

You may want to add your own questions to this list, but these provide a helpful screen to make for less contaminated motives.

Imagine this scene: We're thrilled to be invited as guests to the wedding banquet that God has prepared for us (Matthew 22). We're always worried, though, about food preparation, having once had an awful bout of food poisoning. So, as a precaution, we bring our own brown bag with some munchies that we've carefully prepared. As a result, we deprive ourselves of enjoying God's banquet to the fullest and we insult our host. How can we for a moment think our worries about the contamination of sin should remain a problem in God's presence, when He took care of that on the cross? It's eating what *we* bring to the party that causes the problems, not what our host provides.

See also **Ambition [43]; Doubts [48].**

Three Different Approaches

FIRST, we could err on the side of being convinced that our sinful lives will prevent us from knowing and living out God's will, and therefore neglect the potential He's given us to hear His voice. That's the strategy of never eating again because you're terrified of contaminated food. Oliver R. Barclay provides a sensible corrective: "[I]t is no good indulging in endless introspection. We must make allowances for our own selfishness and get on."[2]

SECOND, we can neglect our sinful natures and fool ourselves into thinking that any prompting must be from the Lord, that any leading we sense is free and untainted by our motives. That approach is like ignoring basic safeguards in how we handle and prepare our food.

THE THIRD way is to go ahead embracing both these realities, but ensuring that God's outworking in our lives has the upper hand. That means practicing decision making while trusting God to play the aces that will trump our mixed motives. Having carefully and honestly recognized what our selfish interests in any decision may be, we can move ahead confident that we'll clearly see God's purposes for us. That approach is like exercising plain common sense in cooking a burger long enough to wipe out the e-coli. We're aware of the dangers but use our good judgment in addressing them head on—and get on with enjoying the meal.

55 The Scrooge Pitfall

The perverse notion that we should enjoy no good things from God is a warped view of His love for us, and offers us only the reward of a deluded self-righteousness.

Paul Little on Acting Like Scrooge . . .

So many of us see God as a kind of celestial Scrooge who peers over the balcony of heaven trying to find anybody who is enjoying life. And when he spots a happy person, he yells, "Now cut that out!" That concept of God should make us shudder because it's blasphemous.[3]

It's hard to know what causes the kind of thinking among Christians that leads us to see God as a spoiler, a killjoy. Is it perhaps our incomplete view of God, in which we see Him as a God of wrath, ready at any moment to strike down anyone for disobedience? It is hopelessly distorted logic that leads us to view human existence as the following sequence:

People sin because they think it will bring them enjoyment.

Sin displeases God.

Therefore all enjoyment must be avoided.

This kind of thinking isn't new. Derek Tidball writes that "Some killjoys in the New Testament were trying to teach that if you were truly following God, you would have to lead a miserable life."[4] Tidball says Paul responded to this situation in

1 Timothy 4:4-5, where the apostle tried to correct this misunderstanding in the early church. It doesn't take long to figure out the silliness of this reasoning that has been with us since the church's earliest days.

Our view of guidance is nevertheless often marred by this approach. We fear that if God is calling us to something we'd enjoy, that somehow we must have a wrong signal—that He couldn't possibly be allowing that to happen. God wants us to avoid the temptations of ego, of "living in the flesh," or of not living disciplined, sacrificial lives. He will therefore guide us only into situations that we would not naturally have preferred. To enjoy our work, for example, may tempt us to move it to idol status in our lives, and we all know that our joy is to come only from the Lord Himself. Hence, it is only by being miserable at work that we can fully know God's joy in our lives.

You see how nonsensical this gets. It's important to counter this tendency by turning to Scripture, which presents a totally different picture of God's infinite care and love for us. For example, Jeremiah 29:11 says: "'For I know the plans I have for you,' declares the LORD, 'plans to prosper you and not to harm you, plans to give you hope and a future.'" Or Romans 8:32: "He who did not spare his own Son, but gave him up for us all—how will he not also, along with him, graciously give us all things?" These and other verses describe a God whose character is the polar opposite of the Scrooge-like being we may put in God's place.

God is not some kind of "ascetic who delights in saying no," as J. Oswald Sanders puts it. So, before we start attributing to this God of grace the qualities of a mean-spirited bureaucrat who will let us do nothing that might bring us joy, let's be clear on the basics. Quoting from Romans 12:2, Tidball concludes that God's total design for our lives is "good, pleasing and perfect." Embrace His will for us with confidence and gratitude, Tidball says, "And enjoy it, without guilt."

See also **The "Abba, Father" Principle [18]; Guilt [50].**

56 Worry

Like guilt, worry is a pointless, unbiblical activity that reflects a lack of trust in God's ability and readiness to guide us.

Worry is the fear that something bad may happen, and—even worse—that I won't be able to do anything about it. Two problems are associated with worry. The first is that it reflects a natural but nevertheless clear lack of faith in God's ability and willingness to meet our needs. The second is that it's a negative and damaging force in our spiritual walk, which will hinder our ability to make godly decisions.

Like **Indecision [52]**, worry has some limited value: that of prodding us into positive action. Most of us though, don't use worry in that way. We turn to worry for comfort or answers, yet by itself it gives us neither. Rather, we should return to the basics of our faith: that we have a God whose parent-like love for us is infinite. Rooted in

> ## Lacking Trust
>
> All worry is atheism, because it is a want of trust in God.
>
> —Fulton Sheen

that reality, we can address our problems and difficulties with the renewed confidence that God is in charge, and that in His good time He'll let us know what He has in mind. In other words, we must in the meanwhile get on with what we know to do right now, and not be deflected by the pointless counter-productivity of worrying about what might need to be done tomorrow.

As the old slogan goes, "Why worry?" Two reasons come to mind, neither of which holds water for the Christian. The first is that we don't know what might happen next, and that bothers us. Well, that's not our problem—or in fact a problem at all—if God's in charge of tomorrow. (See **The Future [23]**.) For the person who's fully committed to Christ, and who entrusts his or her future fully to an all-powerful, all-loving, and all-knowing God, what exactly *is* there to worry about? The second is that some grim stuff may lie ahead. Maybe it's the serious illness you are facing, the loss of a job, or some other potentially devastating news. "How will I cope?" we ask ourselves. Here, too, the answer for the Christian is rooted in the God of Scripture, not in worry.

Never once in Scripture do we get even a hint of Jesus worrying about anything. He always was clear on what His Father wanted Him to do next. Nor did He spend time in worry when facing the horror of the cross. He wrestled in prayer in Gethsemane, asking that this cup be taken away if at all possible, but affirming a commitment to unswerving obedience to His Father's will. For us too, even when we are at the Gethsemane points in our lives, let's not turn to worry when we should be turning to God Himself. If there are things to be done, God will show us what they are; and if there's nothing to be done but go through the worst that life can bring us, He will walk beside us as we draw on His grace so that we may endure. Donald J. Morgan said, "Every evening I turn my troubles over to God—he's going to be up all night anyway."[5]

See also **Waiting [40].**

> ### Don't Worry, Be Cared For
>
> Cast all your anxiety on him because he cares for you.
> —1 Peter 5:7

Running Toward Obedience

Obedience is not a stodgy plodding in the ruts of religion, it is a hopeful race toward God's promises.

Eugene Peterson

Putting Guidance to Work

57 Obedience

Finding out what God wants you to do and not doing it leaves you even worse off than if you'd not learned His will in the first place.

If we're honest, most of the time our problem isn't trying to discover God's will, it's *doing* it. (See **The Ninety-Nine Percent Rule [26].**) Beyond that, there's not much to be said. We could spend time looking at various reasons why we don't do what we know God has called us to, whether it concerns His general or specific will for our lives. We could look at the nature of the temptations we face and why we succumb to them; we could reflect on our lack of **Courage [47],** or our predisposition to choose a sinful path rather than a holy one.

Willing to Obey?

"Why do you call me 'Lord, Lord,' and do not do what I say?"

—Luke 6:46

But none of this takes us beyond the fundamental point we already know: "This is the way; walk in it" (Isaiah 30:21).

See also **The Ambassador Principle [19]; Excuses, Excuses [32].**

58 Pulling Up in Unbelief (or Post-Cognitive Dissonance)

Resist the temptation to pull up in unbelief what you planted in faith.

"Post-cognitive Dissonance" is a psychological term that describes the discomfort or doubts we often experience after making a major decision. If you've just committed to buying a new car, for example, you're likely to worry about whether you've bought the right brand, paid a fair price, chosen the right options, and so on. You may have heard this called "Buyer's Remorse." The many aspects of this extensively researched concept don't concern us here, but the basic idea provides a helpful insight on guidance. Second guessing your decision is a normal, natural thing to do. Millions of people around the world each day make major decisions and then wonder if they've done the right thing.

How should we approach this perfectly natural tendency to reconsider decisions as soon as they've been made? The first thing is to recognize that we're not immune to this phenomenon. Expect that you're highly likely to have second thoughts or misgivings. So, don't be surprised if a whole gaggle of question marks and second guesses show up at your house and stand on the lawn murmuring doubts that get you questioning your decision.

The second thing to note is that these unwanted guests in your yard deserve firm treatment. It's important to shoo them away before they settle down and become part of your landscape.

> ### Immediate Obedience!
>
> At once they left their nets and followed him.
> —Mark 1:18

> ### Fit to Serve?
>
> An office-bearer who wants something other than to obey his King is unfit to bear his office.
> —Abraham Kuyper

J. Oswald Sanders on Unbelief . . .

Having come to a . . . prayerful decision after having renounced personal preference and prejudice, there is no reason to review or question your guidance. *Never dig up in unbelief what you have sown in faith.* Begin with the confidence that God will guide, and end with the assurance that he has guided.

If your decision flows out of **The Big Five [1]** and you've brought to the guidance process a genuine commitment to seeking God's will and the other points listed in **Conditional Guidance [21]**, then you can set aside your Post-cognitive Dissonance and confidently move ahead.

See also **Doubts [48]**.

59 When Guidance "Goes Wrong"

Knowing that God doesn't make mistakes makes it hard to accept when His guidance seemingly brings hurt, failure, or unhappiness; learning why can be just as hard.

When guidance seems to "go wrong" in some way, we're driven to ask why. Often there are no clear answers. The seven points below can help us think through both what has happened and, most important, what needs to happen next.

Expect guidance to lead to results that differ from what you expected. Be careful not to hold unrealistic expectations about how life will be now that God has clearly guided you on a particular issue. No matter what area of life we're talking about, guidance is simply telling you which road to

> ### Three Promises
>
> Jesus promised his disciples three things: that they would be completely fearless, absurdly happy, and in constant trouble.
>
> —F. R. Maltby

take: It's not a prediction of traffic conditions or road hazards. (See **Testing, Testing [16]; Doubts [48]; Worry [56].**)

When the unpleasant surprises come, it's natural to ask if you misunderstood God's guidance in the first place, or whether this is simply a time of testing as you live out in obedience exactly what you should be doing. Let's say you've moved your family to a new city to take up an exciting new position, but you find yourself jobless when the company goes bankrupt six weeks after you get to town. Is this a result of mistaken guidance on your part, perhaps because you too eagerly read what you wanted into God's leading? Or is this one of those tough times when you simply need to accept that God knew exactly what He was doing and that you just don't see the bigger picture quite yet? As best you can, try to determine if your present difficulty is because of your mistake or simply a normal outworking of doing what God wants you to. Go back and review the guidance process you went through. But if you don't have a good reason to believe that you've taken a wrong step, why are you now doubting the validity of the guidance you received? (See **Pulling Up in Unbelief [58].**)

> ## The Testing of Faith
>
> Consider it pure joy, my brothers, whenever you face trials of many kinds, because you know that the testing of your faith develops perseverance.
>
> —James 1:2-3

J. I. Packer on Trouble . . .

The wise person will take opportunity from new troubles to check the original guidance carefully. Trouble should always be treated as a call to consider one's ways. But trouble is not necessarily a sign of being off track at all: for . . . the Bible declares in general that "many are the afflictions of the righteous."

What if I did make some mistake in understanding God's guidance? That could happen for various reasons, such as being in too much of a hurry, or failing to set aside our self-ishness because of the **Mixed Motives [54]** that inevitably mark our decision making. The reason isn't nearly as important as what we do next. Having recognized that we didn't rely on God's leading as we should have, confession is the next step. Then we must turn to God the alchemist, who can take whatever elements now mark our situation and transform them into something new. We can take comfort from Keith Miller, who writes, "[F]or a Christian, *nothing* is wasted in this life: no bad decision, no vocational change, no personal failure." The God who showed Ezekiel that He could bring dead bones to life can turn the worst of our circumstances into good.

Whatever mistakes we may have made, God's redemptive power can override even the worst of our blunders. Think of God as the ultimate highway engineer, capable of building an instant on-ramp for us any time we steer off the highway He's told us to travel. Whether it's a guidance issue or anything else, if we're off track God is always standing by to pave the way for us to return to the way we should go. As long as we're walking in His way, we can with confidence hand over every aspect of our lives to Him—even those that lie in chaos because of our wrongdoing. In the long run, we know Ugo Betti is correct when he says, "To believe in God is to know that all the rules will be fair and that there will be wonderful surprises."[1]

If we erred and "misread" God's guidance, what lessons should we learn from our mistake? Making mistakes in our Christian walk is normal and natural. And if we're honest and don't sug-arcoat things, we're either talking about sinful conduct or the limitations of our sinful natures. Not hearing God as well as we should arises from our flaws, not from God's deficiencies as a communicator. What's important here is to recognize the need to move ahead and to learn from our mistakes. God isn't surprised by our mistakes and failures. Nor should we be surprised when we make our next one. A key lesson is to make new mistakes; if we keep making the same ones over and over again we're showing God we're willfully deaf to what He wants to teach us.

> ## God's Love Wins Out
>
> He will never let us go, he will always recall us. His covenant love will always outwit our sinful stupidity any day.
>
> —Dennis Lennon[2]

While you might expect that disobeying God would have unwelcome consequences, so too must we expect that obedience could bring us hardship and trouble. Don't be surprised when following God's guidance leads you to unexpected potholes, twists, or turns in the road, or alarmingly heavy traffic during a thunderstorm. Jesus' obedience, for example, led Him to the cross. As His disciples, we too are called to take up our cross and follow Him. Nowhere in Scripture does Jesus even hint that a life of obedience equates to a life of ease and comfort. If anything, facing a tough time could well be confirmation that we're doing what God has asked of us. In this context, someone once wrote: "The Lord may not have planned that this should overtake me, but He has most certainly permitted it. Therefore though it were an attack of an enemy, by the time it reaches me, it has the Lord's permission and therefore all is well. He will make it work together with all life's experiences for good."

If we can claim in all humility and confidence that we're on the right path, then it's time simply to seek God's grace to carry us through this rough ride. Now, in **Obedience [57],** we must live out God's calling to us, knowing that He'll ask of us no more than He'll equip us to do. When we're tempted to give up and turn from the way He has shown us, we do well to turn to 1 Corinthians 10:13: "God keeps faith and will not let you be tested beyond your powers, but when the test comes he will at the same time provide a way out and so enable you to endure" (REV).

Discovering why things went wrong isn't nearly as important as finding out what to do next. Sometimes we simply don't know, even after prolonged soul searching, whether it was our misreading of guidance or faithfulness to God's call that has brought us to our present difficulties. That's the time to let go of the past and concentrate on what God wants us to do next. For example, your church might have called a pastor who seemed just right—and for whom your church had searched with great prayer. The church was unanimous in believing this was God's person for you, but now it's plain that it's not a good match. What went wrong? Perhaps despite lengthy analysis of your motives, you'll never know the answer. Instead of remain-

Working for the Good

And we know that in all things God works for the good of those who love him, who have been called according to his purpose.

—Romans 8:28

ing bogged down in examining what happened, it's time to move on and turn again to **The Future [23]**.

See also **Perfect Plans [15]; Five Groundless Fears [49]**.

My Father, teach us not only

your will, but how to do it. Teach us the best way

of doing the best thing, lest we spoil the end by

unworthy means.

J. H. Jowett

Doing Your Best

Finding More Help

*For this God
is our God
for ever and ever;
he will be
our guide
even to the end.*

Psalm 48:14

60 Key Scripture Verses

Listed here are selected Scripture passages on guidance and seeking God's will. They're intended simply as a sampling of the many references in Scripture that speak to God's desire and ability to show us His direction for our lives.

God's Will for Us

Delight yourself in the LORD and he will give you the desires of your heart.
—Psalm 37:4

For we are God's workmanship, created in Christ Jesus to do good works, which God prepared in advance for us to do.
—Ephesians 2:10

Therefore do not be foolish, but understand what the Lord's will is.
—Ephesians 5:17

For this reason . . . we have not stopped praying for you and asking God to fill you with the knowledge of his will through all spiritual wisdom and understanding. And we pray this in order that you may live a life worthy of the Lord and may please him in every way: bearing fruit in every good work, growing in the knowledge of God.
—Colossians 1:9-10

Epaphras . . . is always wrestling in prayer for you, that you may stand firm in all the will of God, mature and fully assured.
—Colossians 4:12

It is God's will that you should be sanctified.
— 1 Thessalonians 4:3

Be joyful always; pray continually; give thanks in all circumstances, for this is God's will for you in Christ Jesus.
— 1 Thessalonians 5:16-18

Promises of God's Guidance and Plans for Us

Then Job replied to the LORD, "I know that you can do all things; no plan of yours can be thwarted."
—Job 42:1-2

He guides the humble in what is right and teaches them his way.
—Psalm 25:9

I will instruct you and teach you in the way you should go; I will counsel you and watch over you.
—Psalm 32:8

If the LORD delights in a man's way, he makes his steps firm; though he stumble, he will not fall, for the LORD upholds him with his hand.
—Psalm 37:23-24

You guide me with your counsel, and afterward you will take me into glory.
—Psalm 73:24

Trust in the LORD with all your heart and lean not on your own understanding; in all your ways acknowledge him, and he will make your paths straight.
—Proverbs 3:5-6

[W]isdom is found in those who take advice.
—Proverbs 13:10

The LORD Almighty has sworn, "Surely as I have planned, so it will be, and as I have purposed, so it will stand."
—Isaiah 14:24

Whether you turn to the right or to the left, your ears will hear a voice behind you, saying, "This is the way; walk in it."
—Isaiah 30:21

The LORD will guide you always; he will satisfy your needs in a sun-scorched land and will strengthen your frame. You will be like a well-watered garden, like a spring whose waters never fail.
—Isaiah 58:11

"For I know the plans I have for you," declares the LORD, "plans to prosper you and not to harm you, plans to give you hope and a future."
—Jeremiah 29:11

"Ask and it will be given to you; seek and you will find; knock and the door will be opened to you."
—Matthew 7:7

When Jesus spoke again to the people, he said, "I am the light of the world. Whoever follows me will never walk in darkness, but will have the light of life."
—John 8:12

"But when he, the Spirit of truth, comes, he will guide you into all truth."
—John 16:13

*If any of you lacks wisdom, he should ask God, who gives generously to all
without finding fault, and it will be given to him.*
—James 1:5

On Ignoring God's Will

*"Woe betide the rebellious children!" says the Lord, "who make plans, but not of my devising, who
weave schemes, but not inspired by me, so piling sin on sin. Without consulting me they hurry
down to Egypt to seek shelter under Pharaoh's protection."*
—Isaiah 30:1-2 (REV)

Individual Encounters with the Will of God

Moses
So now, go. I am sending you to Pharaoh to bring my people the Israelites out of Egypt.
—Exodus 3:10

Joshua
*Have I not commanded you? Be strong and courageous. Do not be terrified; do not be
discouraged, for the LORD your God will be with you wherever you go.*
—Joshua 1:9

Gideon
*The LORD turned to [Gideon] and said, "Go in the strength you have and save Israel out of
Midian's hand. Am I not sending you?"*
—Judges 6:14

Samson's Mother
*The angel of the Lord appeared to her and said, "You are sterile and childless,
but you are going to conceive and have a son."*
—Judges 13:3

Samuel

The LORD came and stood there, calling as at the other times, "Samuel! Samuel!"
Then Samuel said, "Speak, for your servant is listening."
—1 Samuel 3:10

Esther

When Esther's words were reported to Mordecai, he sent back this answer:
"Do not think that because you are in the king's house you alone of all the Jews will escape. . . .
And who knows but that you have come to royal position for such a time as this?"
Then Esther sent this reply to Mordecai: "Go, gather together all the
Jews who are in Susa, and fast for me.
Do not eat or drink for three days, night or day. I and my maids will fast as you do.
When this is done I will go to the king, even though it is against the law."
—Esther 4:12-15

Isaiah

Then I head the voice of the Lord saying, "Whom shall I send? And who will go for us?"
And I said, "Here am I. Send me!"
—Isaiah 6:8

Jeremiah

"Ah, Sovereign LORD," I said, "I do not know how to speak; I am only a child."
But the LORD said to me, "Do not say, 'I am only a child.' You must go to everyone
I send you to and say whatever I command you. Do not be afraid of them,
for I am with you and will rescue you," declares the LORD.
—Jeremiah 1:6-7

Jonah

The word of the LORD came to Jonah son of Amittai: "Go to the great city of Nineveh
and preach against it, because its wickedness has come up before me."
—Jonah 1:1-2

Mary

But the angel said to her, "Do not be afraid, Mary, you have found favor with God. You will give
birth to a son, and you are to give him the name Jesus."
—Luke 1:30-31

Joseph

*When they had gone, an angel of the Lord appeared to Joseph in a dream.
"Get up," he said, "take the child and his mother and escape to Egypt. Stay there until
I tell you, for Herod is going to search for the child to kill him."*
—Matthew 2:13

Jesus

*"Abba, Father," he said, "everything is possible for you. Take this cup from me.
Yet not what I will, but what you will."*
—Mark 14:36

Saul

*"Who are you, Lord?" Saul asked. "I am Jesus, whom you are persecuting," he replied.
"Now get up and go into the city, and you will be told what you must do."*
—Acts 9:5-6

Ananias

*In Damascus there was a disciple named Ananias. The Lord called to him in
a vision, "Ananias!" "Yes, Lord," he answered. The Lord told him,
"Go to the house of Judas on Straight Street and ask for a man from
Tarsus named Saul, for he is praying."*
—Acts 9:10-11

61 Prayers

A Selection of Prayers to Help in Choosing Well

God of all goodness, grant us to desire ardently, to seek wisely, to know surely
and to accomplish perfectly thy holy will, for the glory of thy name.
—Thomas Aquinas

Father, I am seeking,
I am hesitant and uncertain, but will you, O God,
watch over each step of mine and guide me.
—St. Augustine

Holy Spirit think through me till your ideas are my ideas.
—Amy Carmichael

Lord, let thy glory be my end, thy word my rule, and then thy will be done.
—King Charles II of England

Save us, O Lord, from the snares of a double mind.
Deliver us from all cowardly neutralities.
Make us to go in the paths of your commandments,
and to trust for our defense in your almighty arm alone,
through Jesus Christ our Lord.
—Richard Froude[1]

Take my will and make it thine;
It shall be no longer mine:
Take my heart, it is thine own;
It shall be thy royal throne.
—Frances Ridley Havergal

Teach us, Lord,
to serve you as you deserve,
to give and not to count the cost,
to fight and not to heed the wounds,
to toil and not to seek for rest,
to labor and not to seek for any reward
save that of knowing that we do your will.
—St. Ignatius of Loyola

O Lord, you know what is best for us; let this or that be done,
as you shall please. Give what you will, and how much you will,
and when you will. Deal with me as you think best, and as best
pleases you. Set me where you will, and deal with me
in all things just as you will. Behold, I am your servant, prepared for
all things; for I desire not to live unto myself, but unto you; and oh,
that I could do it worthily and perfectly!
—Thomas à Kempis

O my Lord, how obvious it is that you are almighty! There is no
need to understand the reasons for your commands. So long as we
love and obey you, we can be certain that you will direct us on to
the right path. And as we tread that path, we will know that it is
your power and love that has put us there.
—Teresa of Ávila

62 Resources

The book you are now holding is deeply indebted to ideas culled from many other works on guidance and God's will. Here are some that will provide useful further reading.

Elisabeth Elliot. *God's Guidance: A Slow and Certain Light.* Old Tappan, NJ: Fleming Revell, 1972. A particularly thoughtful and wide-ranging overview of guidance, now available in an updated edition with a study guide.

Gary Friesen. *Decision Making and the Will of God.* Portland, Ore.: Multnomah, 1980. This is a scholarly, richly researched analysis of what Scripture says about God and our decision making. While lengthy and not easygoing, it's still a valuable tool for serious digging into what the Bible says about guidance and decision making.

Gloria Gaither. *Decisions: A Christian's Approach to Making Right Choices.* Waco, Texas: Word, 1982. As the title suggests, this personal, easy-to-read volume concentrates on decision making but addresses various other aspects of guidance as well.

Phillip Jensen and Tony Payne. *The Last Word on Guidance.* Kingsford, Australia, London: St. Matthias Press, 1991. Despite the arrogant sounding title, this book emphasizes understanding God's character and will as the foundation for (and "the last word on") all guidance.

Ron Kincaid. *Praying for Guidance.* Downers Grove, Ill.: InterVarsity, 1996. This book covers a wide range of prayer-related issues concerning guidance and offers many valuable insights on this aspect of The Big Five.

Paul Little. *Affirming the Will of God.* Downers Grove, Ill.: InterVarsity, 1971. This classic booklet is a superb summary of all the main principles of guidance. Only 31 pages, it's a quick read and surprisingly comprehensive. It's no surprise InterVarsity keeps reprinting this gem.

J. I. Packer. *Finding God's Will.* Downers Grove, Ill.: InterVarsity, 1985. Another concise contribution, this booklet is an excerpt from Packer's book, *Knowing God.* A straightforward, quick introduction to the topic.

J. Oswald Sanders. *Every Life a Plan of God.* Grand Rapids: Discovery House, 1992. This book offers a common sense approach to the issue of whether God has a detailed, ideal plan for each of His children. It includes much helpful advice, especially on making difficult decisions.

Gerald L. Sittser. *The Will of God as a Way of Life.* Grand Rapids: Zondervan, 2000. This book makes the important point that we need to be living out God's will in our lives in the present. God's will, he says, "has to do with what we already know, not what we must figure out."

M. Blaine Smith. *Knowing God's Will*, 2nd edition. Downers Grove, Ill.: InterVarsity, 1991. A wonderfully thorough, thoughtful overview of the main issues; this volume has entered a second edition and has sold more than 100,000 copies.

John Stott. *The Contemporary Christian*. Downers Grove, Ill.: InterVarsity, 1992. This excellent book contains a chapter focusing on Guidance, Vocation, and Ministry that packs in considerable insight on these three related areas.

Charles R. Swindoll. *The Mystery of God's Will*. Nashville: Word, 1999. Swindoll, in his easy-reading, conversational style, grapples with the hard questions facing anyone seriously seeking God's will.

Derek Tidball. *How Does God Guide?* London: Collins, 1990. A comprehensive, readable overview of the main issues.

Bruce Waltke. *Finding the Will of God: A Pagan Notion?* Gresham, Ore.: Vision House, 1995. Waltke argues in this provocatively titled book that we need to redefine the way we think about God's will. We should focus more on what Scripture teaches about "following God's program of guidance" rather than obsessing over divination-like strategies for "finding His will."

Dallas Willard. *Hearing God*. Downers Grove, Ill.: InterVarsity, 1999. (Previously published as *In Search of Guidance.*) This book's emphasis, to quote the subtitle, is on "developing a conversational relationship with God." In other words, we're likely to struggle to know God's will unless we're in an ongoing, healthy relationship with Him.

Alphabetical List of Topics

The "Abba, Father" Principle
God's guidance is that of a loving, involved parent who seeks nothing but our best. Pages 75-77

Advice
Always seek the advice of mature Christians to affirm and confirm what you think God is telling you. Pages 34-36

The Ambassador Principle
Christians who take seriously Paul's view that we are ambassadors for Christ must be ready to act upon new orders to move to another posting at short notice. Pages 77-78

Ambition—An Uneasy Path
Few of us succeed in balancing our desires for advancement and success while letting God have His way; ambition is packed with potential for deluding ourselves about God's will. Pages 131-136

Asking the Right Questions
Work on asking the right questions; avoid those that are already settled, pointless, or irrelevant. Pages 45-46

The Big Five—and Beyond

Every quest for guidance should be shaped by scriptural guidelines, prayer, the advice of other Christians, the circumstances we face, and an overall sense that this course is what God wants. Pages 17, 23-25

Calling

Don't confuse a "need" with a "call"—needs are plentiful, calls are few, and calls that God makes of you are few indeed. Pages 137-140

Change

Change is at the heart of guidance, which by definition means God brings us to a point where we must embrace or resist a new step in our lives. If you're uncomfortable about change, prepare for what could be a rough ride. Pages 46-49

Choices, Choices

Not all choices are created equal; some are between good and bad options, others between good and equally good, and yet others are so minor that they really don't matter. Pages 78-82

Circumstances

While never the final word, circumstances can help us sort through the authentic and unreliable messages we may get in the guidance process. Pages 37-39

The Clarity Principle

If you can't state in one sentence the issue on which you're seeking guidance, work on clarifying the destination before continuing the trip. Pages 101-102

Clear Thinking

We don't serve a mindless God, and He expects us to mirror that part of His character by using our intellect to think through questions of guidance. Pages 49-53

Conditional Guidance

God's guidance isn't like a legal contract, but it still comes with conditions; read the bold print about what He expects of us. Pages 82-84

The Consistency Principle

While we can never predict exactly how God may guide, we know His guidance will never contradict His Word or character. Pages 84-85

Courage
Expect decision making to be a difficult, sometimes anguished process that may demand courageous action, but we are assured by God Himself that He will empower and sustain us at every step. Pages 147-148

The Default Strategy
Choosing a default position by deciding to do something unless God tells you otherwise can help clarify where He's leading you. Pages 102-104

Do What You Like
God normally calls us to tasks that fit our gifts and which we're likely to enjoy, especially when it involves our work. Assuming that we should do what we already like is a good place to begin. Pages 104-107

Doors — Open and Closed
Closed doors don't mean God never wants you to enter; open ones don't mean you should. (Or, before trying a door, see what you can learn by looking through a window.) Pages 53-57

Doubts
Expect and welcome doubts in guidance, but when you've made a decision, know that their work is done. Pages 148-150

Equipping the Called
God calls some He has already equipped and will equip all others whom He has called. Pages 141-142

Excuses, Excuses
Don't avoid God's call with excuses and false humility; His harshest answer to you is that He may ask someone else to do His work. Page 107

Five Groundless Fears
Beware of groundless fears that can keep you from finding and living out God's will. Pages 151-154

Fleeces
Using Gideon's strategy of laying out a fleece isn't necessarily a bad idea, but it isn't a particularly good one either. Pages 108-112

Flipping a Coin
While there's biblical precedent for this kind of decision making in guidance,

it's both a last resort and tough to imagine Jesus doing. Pages 112-113

Formation Flying
The Christian life isn't a solo enterprise; God guides us in keeping with His will for the church and His kingdom. Pages 113-114

The Future
Guidance is, by definition, concerned with the future, but with only one piece at a time. Pages 85-86

Getting Ready for Guidance
Be at work now cultivating those qualities that will enable God to guide you more easily in the future. Pages 87-89

Godly Decision Making
Anyone can make decisions; what God expects of us are decisions that are made with Him and His kingdom in mind. Pages 114-116

God's Will — General and Specific
We already know plenty about God's general will, but little about His specific will — and confusing the two can be, well, confusing. Pages 89-94

Guidance in a Crunch
When you have to make a choice quickly, remember that here, too, the guidance-seeking principles remain the same: Go back to the basics of **The Big Five.** Pages 116-119

Guilt
Guilt is a negative, obstructionist force in seeking God's will and can easily seduce us from the paths we should follow. Pages 154-155

How God Guides — Using "The Stuff of This World"
While we can never predict the specifics of how God will guide in any given situation, we can be sure He will lead us far more often through means that are ordinary and pre-dictable rather than spectacular. Pages 57-59

Hubris — Christian Style
Beware of assuming too easily that we can do anything we think God has called us to do. Not only can we do nothing on our own, we need to be

certain we've heard correctly in the first place. Pages 155-156

Indecision (or The Paralysis of Analysis)

Remember the difference between thorough, thoughtful processing of The Big Five, and sustained dithering and indecisiveness that brings no honor to God. Pages 156-157

Inner Peace

Inner peace is necessary, but by itself is not a sufficient condition for choosing a course of action. Pages 39-41

Intuition and Feelings

Intuition and feelings have a part to play in the guidance process, but the more you prize them the less value they have. Pages 59-60

Key Scripture Verses

Various verses on guidance and knowing God's will are included in this section. Pages 179-184

The Law of Unintended Consequences

Taking ill-advised action can set in motion a spiritual chain reaction that

you may greatly regret. Pages 157-159

Listening

Frank Laubach's advice on prayer is no more applicable than when we're seeking guidance: "Listening to God is far more important than giving him your ideas." Pages 59-64

Maturity

As we grow in our faith, God expects us to mature in how we seek His guidance. Pages 64-66

Mixed Motives

Even though our sinful natures make it impossible to act from pure motives, being aware of this as we seek God's leading will itself reduce the contamination. Pages 159-161

The Need Versus the Call

It's important to distinguish between the needs in the world God undoubtedly wants addressed, and those to which He's calling you. Pages 142-143

The Ninety-Nine Percent Rule

Ninety-nine percent of the time we already know God's will, and the

problem is living it out; it's for the other one percent of the time that we need His guidance.
Pages 94-95

Obedience
Finding out what God wants you to do and not doing it leaves you even worse off than if you'd not learned His will in the first place.
Pages 169-170

The "Pain and Problems" Principle
We're more open to guidance when things are going badly in our lives.
Pages 119-120

Perfect Plans
While God's plans are perfect, His love, patience, and boundless imagination lead Him to redraw those plans for our lives whenever necessary.
Pages 66-67

Prayer
Like the other elements in **The Big Five,** prayer is crucial, but by itself is not a sufficient ingredient for knowing God's will. Pages 29-34

Prayers
A selection of prayers to help you choose well are included in this section.
Pages 184-186

Pulling Up in Unbelief (or Post-Cognitive Dissonance)
Resist the temptation to pull up in unbelief what you planted in faith.
Pages 170-171

Resources
Fifteen helpful resources on guidance are included in this section.
Pages 186-188

Scripture
Scripture is a foundational and sufficient basis for the general principles of Christian living. For the particulars of our daily lives we may need to supplement its directions with the other elements in **The Big Five.** Pages 26-29

The Scrooge Pitfall
The perverse notion that we should enjoy no good things from God is a warped view of His love for us, and offers us only the reward of a deluded self-righteousness. Pages 162-163

Signs and Wonders

God normally works in ordinary ways to tell us what He wants us to know; seeking the extraordinary reflects our lack of faith, not its depth. Pages 120-123

Testing, Testing

If what seems like guidance is indeed from God, it can stand testing. Pages 67-69

Trivial Pursuit

While God wants us to have warm feet, we're in danger of insulting Him when we seek His counsel on the color of socks we should wear today. Pages 95-96

Unneeded Guidance

Sometimes we waste our time seeking guidance when God has already shown us what we need to know. Pages 96-97

Waiting

Waiting for God's leading is extraordinarily difficult and unnatural, but always worthwhile. Pages 123-125

What Would Jesus Do?

What better question to ask if we want to be like Him? Page 126

When Guidance "Goes Wrong"

Knowing that God doesn't make mistakes makes it hard to accept when His guidance seemingly brings hurt, failure, or unhappiness; learning why can be just as hard. Pages 171-175

Wisdom

Godly wisdom—knowing what God would have us do next—is a synonym for guidance. Pages 69-71

"Wit's End" Guidance

When you're on the edge of despair and have no sense whatever which direction to pursue, clinging to God's grace will suffice until you can once again think about thinking, guidance, and deciding. Pages 126-128

Worry

Like guilt, worry is a pointless, unbiblical activity that reflects a lack of trust in God's ability and readiness to guide us. Pages 163-165

Notes

Approaching Guidance Issues

1. Hannah Whitall Smith, *The Christian's Secret of a Happy Life* (Westwood, N.J.: Fleming Revell, 1952), p. 94.
2. Max Anders, *30 Days to Understanding How to Live as a Christian* (Dallas: Word, 1994), p. 322.
3. G. Campbell Morgan, *God's Perfect Will* (New York: Fleming Revell, 1901), pp. 156-157.
4. Bruce Waltke, *Finding the Will of God: A Pagan Notion?* (Gresham, Ore.: Vision House, 1995), pp. 31-32.
5. Hannah Whitall Smith, pp. 94-95.
6. G. Christie Swain, quoted in *Quotes for the Journey, Wisdom for the Way*, compiled by Gordon S. Jackson (Colorado Springs: NavPress, 2000), p. 126.
7. G. Campbell Morgan, p. 158.
8. Bruce Dunn, "How Does God Guide?" Sermon delivered at Grace Presbyterian Church, Peoria, Ill., no date, p. 6.
9. Bruce Waltke, p. 148.

Knowing the Basics

1. David Watson, *Grow and Flourish: A Daily Guide to Personal Renewal* (Wheaton, Ill.: Harold Shaw, 1988), p. 223.
2. Derek Tidball, *How Does God Guide?* (London: Collins, 1990), p. 37.
3. All references from M. Blaine Smith are taken from his book *Knowing God's Will* (Downers Grove, Ill.: InterVarsity, 1991).
4. Bruce Waltke, *Finding the Will of God: A Pagan Notion?* (Gresham, Ore.: Vision House, 1995), p. 154.
5. Hannah Whitall Smith, *The Christian's Secret of a Happy Life* (Westwood, N.J.: Fleming Revell, 1952), p. 99.
6. G. Campbell Morgan, *God's Perfect Will* (New York: Fleming Revell, 1901), p. 161.
7. G. Campbell Morgan, p. 159.
8. Paul Little, *Affirming the Will of God* (Downers Grove, Ill.: InterVarsity, 1971), p.16.
9. Yale Kneeland, quoted in Robert Coles, *The Call of Stories: Teaching and the Moral Imagination* (Boston: Houghton Mifflin, 1989), p. 94.
10. Charles Martin, "Daily Bread" Bible reading notes, Dec. 13, 1995 (Wayne, Pa.: Scripture Union, 1995).
11. William McGill, quoted in *Quotes for the Journey, Wisdom for the Way*, compiled by Gordon S. Jackson (Colorado Springs: NavPress, 2000), p. 124.

Understanding God's Will

1. Phillip Jensen and Tony Payne, *The Last Word on Guidance* (Kingsford, Australia and London: St. Matthias Press, 1991), p. 88.
2. Jensen and Payne, p. 8.
3. Hannah Whitall Smith, *The Christian's Secret of a Happy Life* (Westwood, N.J.: Fleming Revell, 1952), p. 96.
4. Gerald L. Sittser, *The Will of God as a Way of Life* (Grand Rapids: Zondervan, 2000), p. 20.

5. Ron Kincaid, *Praying for Guidance* (Downers Grove, Ill.: InterVarsity, 1996), p. 22.
6. Sarah F. Smiley, quoted in *Quotes for the Journey, Wisdom for the Way*, compiled by Gordon S. Jackson (Colorado Springs: NavPress, 2000), p. 69.
7. Paul Little, *Affirming the Will of God* (Downers Grove, Ill.: InterVarsity, 1971), p. 5.

Making Godly Decisions

1. Ian McLaren, quoted in *Quotes for the Journey, Wisdom for the Way*, compiled by Gordon S. Jackson (Colorado Springs: NavPress, 2000), p. 115.
2. James S. Stewart, quoted in *Quotes for the Journey, Wisdom for the Way*, p. 120.
3. Derek Tidball, *How Does God Guide?* (London: Collins, 1990), pp. 178-179
4. Bruce Waltke, *Finding the Will of God: A Pagan Notion?* (Gresham, Ore.: Vision House, 1995), pp. 124-125.
5. John D. Arnold, *Make Up Your Mind! The Seven Building Blocks to Better Decisions* (New York: AMACOM, 1978).
6. W. T. Purkiser, quoted in *Quotes for the Journey, Wisdom for the Way*, p. 170.
7. Derek Tidball, pp. 36-37.

Understanding Calling and Ambition

1. Kathi Hudson, quoted in *Quotes for the Journey, Wisdom for the Way*, compiled by Gordon S. Jackson (Colorado Springs: NavPress, 2000), p. 170.
2. Derek Tidball, *How Does God Guide?* (London: Collins, 1990), pp. 163-167.
3. Gregory T. Bedell, quoted in *Quotes for the Journey, Wisdom for the Way*, p. 66.

Overcoming Concerns

1. Andrew McNab, commentary on James in *The New Bible Commentary* (London: The Inter-Varsity Fellowship, 1954), p. 1119.

2. Oliver R. Barclay, quoted in J. Oswald Sanders, *Every Life a Plan of God* (Crowborough, England: Highland Books, 1991), p. 98.

3. Paul Little, *Affirming the Will of God* (Downers Grove, Ill.: InterVarsity, 1971), p. 11.

4. Derek Tidball, *How Does God Guide?* (London: Collins, 1990), p. 197.

5. Donald J. Morgan, quoted in *Quotes for the Journey, Wisdom for the Way*, compiled by Gordon S. Jackson (Colorado Springs: NavPress, 2000), p. 125.

Putting Guidance to Work

1. Ugo Betti, quoted in *Quotes for the Journey, Wisdom for the Way*, compiled by Gordon S. Jackson (Colorado Springs: NavPress, 2000), p. 60.

2. Dennis Lennon, quoted in *Quotes for the Journey, Wisdom for the Way*, p. 73.

Finding More Help

1. Richard Froude, quoted in *The Doubleday Prayer Collection*, compiled by Mary Batchelor (New York: Doubleday, 1992), p. 71.

Author

Gordon Jackson is the Associate Dean for Academic Affairs at Whitworth College in Spokane, Washington. Gordon grew up in South Africa, where he worked as a journalist on a news magazine. He received his undergraduate education in South Africa before obtaining a master's in communication at Wheaton College and a doctorate in mass communication at Indiana University. He has taught journalism at Whitworth since 1983. *A Compact Guide to Discovering God's Will* is his fourth book. His book *Quotes for the Journey, Wisdom for the Way* was also published by NavPress.

LITTLE BOOKS FULL OF ENORMOUS WISDOM.

A Compact Guide to the Bible

Gain the maximum benefit from the Bible by understanding what you're reading, seeing the Scriptures' big picture, and learning to see your world from God's point of view.

A Compact Guide to the Bible (Karen Lee-Thorp) $9

A Compact Guide to the Christian Life

A Compact Guide to the Christian Life is an instant source of information on the Christian faith and how it applies to life in the modern world. Explore topics such as prayer, starting a small group, friendship, marriage, money, and much more!

A Compact Guide to the Christian Life (Karen Lee-Thorp) $9

A Compact Guide to Balancing Your Life

This compact guide's reader-friendly format leads you to ideas, tips, and biblical insights of what a balanced life looks like—a balanced life with God in control!

A Compact Guide to Balancing Your Life (Brad Lewis) $9

Get your copies today at your local bookstore, visit our website at www.navpress.com, or call (800) 366-7788 and ask for offer **#6169** or a FREE catalog of NavPress products.

NAVPRESS
BRINGING TRUTH TO LIFE
www.navpress.com

Prices subject to change.